WASTE DETECTIVES 2

THE NEW MISSION TO REMOVE WASTE AT SCALE

BRIAN HOOKER

Author: Brian Hooker

© Brian Hooker 2023

The author has asserted their right to be identified as the authors of this work in accordance with the Copyright, Designs and Patents Act 1988.

All rights reserved. No part of this publication may be reproduced, stored in a retrieval system, or transmitted in any way or by any means, including photocopying or recording, without the written permission of the authors. For permission to publish, distribute or otherwise reproduce this work, please contact the authors at contact@thewastedetectives.com

Copyright of Images:

Figure 1.1: Image by desdemona72 / Shutterstock.com
Figure 1.2: Image by Trueffelpix / Shutterstock.com
Figure 2.1 : Image by Andrey_Popov / Shutterstock.com
Figure 2.2 : @ Brian Hooker
Figure 2.3 : Image by Matej Kastelic / Shutterstock.com
Figure 3.1. Image by Olivier Le Moal / Shutterstock.com
Figure 4.1: Image by aurielaki / Shutterstock.com
Figure 4.2: @ Brian Hooker
Figure 5.1 : @ Brian Hooker
Figure 5.2 : @ Brian Hooker
Figure 5.3 : @ Brian Hooker
Figure 5.4 : @ Brian Hooker
Figure 5.5 : @ Brian Hooker
Figure 5.6 : Image by Boris15 / Shutterstock.com
Figure 5.7 : Image by Jaiz Anuar / Shutterstock.com
Figure 6.1 : Image by Keepsmiling4u / Shutterstock.com
Figure 7.1: Image by Menara Grafis / Shutterstock.com
Figure 7.2: Image by Mari-Leaf / Shutterstock.com
Figure 8.1: Image by Funtap / Shutterstock.com
Figure 9.1: Image by Irina Strelnikova / Shutterstock.com
Figure 10.1: Image by Trueffelpix / Shutterstock.com

Author photos:
Photo of Brian Hooker © Ooh La La by Linda Williams (https://oohlalabylinda.com/)

Cover and Interior Design by FormattedBooks.com

A big thank you to my daughter Nia for giving me time to write the book.

—Brian Hooker

ACKNOWLEDGEMENTS

Edwin Reay
Graham Southorn
John Seddon
Melissa Perri
Richard Moir
Wayne Kenny

CONTENTS

Introduction ix

Chapter 1: The importance of influence 1
Chapter 2: Behaviours of digital leaders in the work 31
Chapter 3: Waste Detectives' Methods 51
Chapter 4: Commercial Reasons to Remove Waste 67
Chapter 5: Knowledge Repository & Information 81
Chapter 6: Maturity Modelling 105
Chapter 7: Pain & Interactions 119
Chapter 8: Connecting All Parts of the
             Change Area on the journey 143
Chapter 9: Product Management 157
Chapter 10: Storytelling 173

References 185
About the author 191

INTRODUCTION

Book Topics

1. Putting on the Strategic Agenda
2. The importance of the Influence
3. Waste Detectives Methods and Techniques (Summary)
4. Knowledge Repository (Idea, Concept, Data, Design)
5. Information from the waste knowledge to act on
6. Decision Making and Acting on the Data
7. Waste Maturity Model
8. Connecting All Parts of the Change Areas on the journey
9. Commercial Reason to Want to Remove Waste
10. Pain and Interactions Language
11. Behaviours
12. Digital minded leaders in the work.
13. Story Telling

WASTE CAN SAP A LARGE PERCENTAGE of an organisation's delivery capacity. Removing it increases agile delivery capacity and the flow of products to customers.

As a chief technology officer (CTO), you are key to the success of the organisation's transformation. You may have already started to find and remove waste via a number of teams, now you are tasked with helping organisations find and remove waste at scale, you'll encounter a number of barriers, not just with internal teams but suppliers too.

The main problems are caused by people moving the blocked work into a blocked status and then effectively ignoring it, often via a general chat update in the daily stand-up.

On top of that, there's often a complete lack of knowledge about the types of waste and blockers and the amount of delivery capacity it saps from teams and tribes. In addition, you'll need to get senior managers onside and influence senior leaders and teams to bring them on the journey with you.

Once you've identified where problems can be found, you can embed a method to combat them and scale them right across an organisation. This book gives you the method.

We'll start by looking at the need to influence senior leaders, via a character called Tony. Considering why some senior leaders simply aren't ready to be influenced. Then move into commercial motivation to remove waste and how it translates to financial discussions.

Some of this is a matter of language; adjusting how you speak about waste in ways that are less tech-speak and more easily understood by senior leaders. It's about using the language of opportunity as opposed to words like waste and lost capacity.

We'll also discuss how to put waste on the strategic agenda, and what to look out for on that part of your journey. All this builds into a store of meaningful management information that can be acted upon. Senior leaders can make interventions in the work to improve performance and capacity.

Once you've identified waste in one area, you'll want to remove more of it at scale. We'll introduce techniques for measuring the maturity of the organisation's ability to find and measure waste and remove some of it via the use of experimentation.

We'll move on to how to tell the story and branding the works of finding waste to be removed to increase capacity. And then there's product management that allows finding and removing waste to be aligned to a vision and a long-term journey. Finally, we'll close with the behaviours and other requirements that senior leaders should adopt.

The methods outlined here are aimed at large organisations because that's where I've spent several years in transformation roles, from system engineering and analysis to coaching. I've seen how they work in software companies of different types, including suppliers of single products and providers of bespoke enterprise solutions.

I've identified a lot of waste and removing it in agile processes has become something of a personal crusade. I get a lot of satisfaction seeing it all come together, especially when reluctant senior leaders see the light and become full-on waste converts.

In order to help more people and organisations, I, along with my co-author Richard Moir, developed a framework that we published as *The Waste Detectives: Methods and techniques to improve flow, increase value and boost profitability in a large-scale transformation.* (You can't miss this book on Amazon because of its bright yellow cover!)

But while *The Waste Detectives* method remains valid, this book takes them into new territory. Because even when you have a solid and proven idea for removing waste, you still need to be able to scale it.

So join me on my mission to remove waste and give your client organisations the best possible chance of increasing capacity.

CHAPTER 1
THE IMPORTANCE OF INFLUENCE

As a chief technology officer (CTO) there is a desire to increase the speed of products to customers, finding and removing waste across the whole organisation, waste detective methods can assist you achieving this goal. However to achieve this goal, there is a need to influence the organisation to use The Waste Detectives Methods.

This chapter will discuss innovations over the years in some large organisations that are now established household brands, but initially these innovations faced resistance until they became the norm for customers. Looking at how you can overcome resistance of wanting to find and remove waste in senior leaders by using influencing techniques to scale The Waste Detectives Methods.

The chapter will then introduce concepts you may want to use with your senior leaders, that would help transition the mindset of keeping work busy rather than keeping people busy.

KEY CONCEPTS

Back in the 1990s, I was out having a beer with some friends when one, Tony, asked where I'd bought my jeans. When I said I'd got them online, Tony was incredulous. He viewed online shopping as a mere passing fad. "No one is going to buy clothes on the internet," he pronounced. But whilst he might have preferred strolling around shops, I wanted something different. And as the history of ecommerce clearly shows, I wasn't alone.

Numerous trends that went on to change the world weren't considered very important by many people at the time, even those in the same industry. At one time, Blockbuster Video had 9,094 rental stores and 83,400 employees but today there is just one store left (in Oregon). There was a time when NetFlix was not on anyone's radar and yet its revenue in 2022 was $31.6 billion. (Netflix's founders famously offered to sell up to Blockbuster but were turned down). The point being that the tide can turn when customers are persuaded to try something new.

In a later chapter, we look at The Waste Detectives Methods, which provides you with a framework to get teams and organisations to start finding waste. The hard part is influencing and convincing an entire organisation of the importance of finding and removing waste at scale and potentially also the suppliers who work with the organisation.

But don't worry, *The Waste Detectives* have been through this journey and we will look at some of our learnings, along with some human characteristics that explain why influencing can be difficult. For many people you speak to, all of this is going to be a new concept. Convincing them to try something new will take time, so you'll have to take it a step at a time. It will be worth it in the end, however, so let's look at a few concepts.

Take it from me, finding and removing waste is always going to be a hard sell, particularly if it stands a chance of making a massive difference. Put yourself in the shoes of senior leaders who, year after year, have listened to consultants telling them they could save thousands of pounds and improve their organisation to boot. It's likely that many of those projects failed. The senior leaders who bought into them, and the employees who had new ideas inflicted on them, now fear and dread the next person that comes along and promises to be different.

This reluctance may linger even if you successfully manage to remove some waste. That's because you can't do it all at once. Some teams might be reaping the benefits but, even then, sceptics may still outnumber the evangelists. What, then, is the art of influencing an entire organisation?

Being able to influence others is an important skill in many areas of business, none more so than sales. One of the world's most successful salespeople is Jordan Belfort, whose life was made into the movie *The Wolf of Wall Street*. In real life, Belfort has a line he uses when he presents at seminars. He instructs members of the audience to "Sell me this pen!". He does this to find out who cares what the customer wants and who goes into selling mode straight away. Those who only "sell" are not interested in solving the customer's problems.

Those that are interested in the customer's problems ask questions such as, "When was the last time you bought a pen?", "What was it like?", and "How much did you pay?". The customers that aren't interested in the conversation can just walk away. This allows the salesperson to spend time promoting the product only to people it appeals to.

Think about that when trying to influence people about waste. Listen to what they want and, if there is an opportunity to solve their problems, tailor your language to address them. This saves time and effort because you only target those who want the solution rather than trying to influence everybody. Some simply don't want to hear your solution.

Unfortunately there's no way around this. You cannot convince everyone. There was no way anyone was going to persuade my friend Tony to buy jeans online. But remember that when it comes to waste, you are on the right side of history. You just need to believe in removing waste as a concept yourself and show that you believe it, otherwise others won't buy in. Some people will then be persuaded but understand that it will take time. (That reminds me, I must ask Tony where he buys his jeans today...).

So who do you need to persuade?

Consider the organisations you work with. Typically, they'll have between hundreds and thousands of employees, third-party suppliers, and potentially up to millions of customers consuming their products. At the moment, around 50% of capacity is being wasted. In order to get that capacity back, you are going to have to convince the majority of the organisation of the need to remove waste and that's a lot of people.

So in order to roll out and scale the removal of waste throughout an organisation, you'll need a sponsor as high up as possible – potentially the change director if there is one. You're also going to have to connect with third-party suppliers. Plus, people on the ground are going to have to believe, with a high level of enthusiasm, that the removal of waste at scale is worth their time. In other words, this isn't yet another one of those previous consultancy ideas that died a death in the transformation journey.

You'll have to convince the majority of the organisation but the sticking point is that some people won't be ready for change. Some of them will have strong muscle memory and will take a while to adapt to new concepts, similar to Tony not wanting to purchase his jeans online.

OVERCOMING RELUCTANCE

Let's fast forward six to nine months or so to the stage where you're starting to land the concept of removing waste within an organisation. The teams on the ground get it and have managed to remove waste using techniques from *The Waste Detectives* and other books.

Note: Would also recommend reading of others works such as those found in :

- Dominica DeGrandis's *Making Work Visible: Exposing Time Theft to Optimize Work & Flow* task switching that adds to the waste as explored in Jill Duff's research.

Through the transformation, you have built the green shoots of belief in removing waste for continuous improvement. You had a purpose or goal that you wanted to achieve: finding and removing waste. You wanted to leave the concept embedded in the organisation, not only to allow continuous improvement and make it perform better, but also to leave your thought leadership. Hopefully this embeds over time to become the DNA of the organisation, wanting to continually improve.

At this point, let's bring Tony back in and imagine yourself as an online clothing retailer in the 1990s. Your goal is to sell jeans to customers over the internet but many people won't bite. It's perceived as scary and something they are not comfortable with. You'll need to work through all the resistance to achieve your business goals.

Let's consider some of Tonys objections. The jeans may be the wrong size, so this service would need to build in a returns system. Likewise, they might not look the same as they do online.

Objections:

- The jeans may not fit. How do I return them?
- What if I am not in when they are delivered?
- The colours might look different to the photo.

Similarly, when it comes to removing waste, you will identify Tonys who are resistant to change, who you should put into your "circle of concern". Then there are those who are open, who are within your "circle of influence". Those in the circle of concern may be Tonys who are just not interested at all. Or they could be super Tonys - not just reluctant but destructive. They want to sink the whole endeavour of finding and removing waste. The old saying of keeping your friends close and your enemies closer springs to mind.

When I created The Waste Detectives Methods of finding and removing waste, I encountered one of these super Tonys. Let's call this character Clive. I would present to teams that, on the whole, were interested in my ideas, but Clive would just come in and try to derail things, at all costs it seemed. Beware of Clives.

What are the types of behaviours you could see from potential Clives? Well, they belittle the concept to senior leaders but offer no alternatives in the form of other experiments. Clives are determined to downplay any concept that isn't theirs. Their ambition in life is purely self gain, not thinking of the wider organisation. Do you know any Clives?

When meeting persons who display the behaviours of either Tonys or Clives then, we can note the behaviours so we track and consider techniques of influence. These persons can hinder the ability to influence the roll out and embedding of the Waste Detective Method through the organisation, a technique that can help identify and aid the journey is to use a diagram like one below. The Tonys and Clives you meet would be in "the circle of concern" that can bring a negative energy and sap the energy to influence across throughout the organisation.

The more persons come on board with the method, over time the circle of concern will reduce and aid the ability to scale Waste Detectives method throughout the organisation.

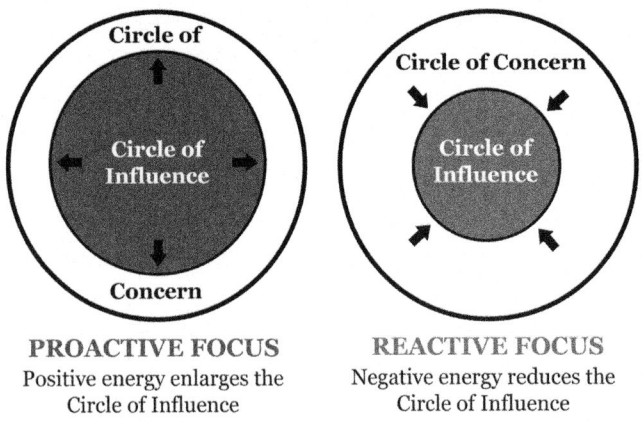

PROACTIVE FOCUS
Positive energy enlarges the
Circle of Influence

REACTIVE FOCUS
Negative energy reduces the
Circle of Influence

Figure 1.1: Circle of Influence and concern.
Image by desdemona72 / Shutterstock.com

Bringing it back to removing waste at scale: you know it works and you know it's the right thing for the organisation and will benefit everyone. But this will be new and scary for many. They'll be unclear what it means to them as individuals and the organisation as a whole. This creates fear. But those on your journey with you are going to need to work without fear. Uncovering waste and problems might, in turn, expose individuals. So as a CTO, you will have agile coaches to support labs and teams in an open-minded and supportive environment.

Areas of leadership work you'll need to own as a CTO leading on finding and removing waste at scale. We'll go on to explore each of these areas in turn.

Figure 1.2: Leadership categories you'll need to own as a change consultant.

Image by Trueffelpix / Shutterstock.com

GUIDANCE

You need to provide consistent guidance and be available for anyone in the organisation to contact you. Supporting them is vital, and listening and working with those on the ground will swell the numbers wanting to help the organisation find and remove waste.

As the number of interested people increases, so will the number of individuals and teams who want direct support. Your available time will decrease as a result and distract you from other areas. This is where you can bring in people with similar interests in the goal and your approach to finding and removing waste.

Later in the book we will look at the finding and removing waste maturity model. This will allow that self-sustaining method, as well as providing a leading measure on how well the organisation is performing at finding and removing waste.

Communication and storytelling, also covered in Chapter 10, are other vital tools in your locker.

SOLUTION

You have successfully managed to implement *The Waste Detectives'* methods and techniques, or other methods, to find and remove waste in a number of teams. However, there are tens, if not hundreds, more teams and capacity is being sapped to the tune of 50%.

In order to get to the goal of finding and removing waste for continuous improvement, all teams must buy into your vision and concept. You'll need the teams using it, liking it, and wanting to use it, and senior leaders wanting to act on the knowledge the teams find in order to remove it via experimentation.

Adapting as you go, whilst at the same time building a scalable, strategic solution, is the balance you have to strike. In the early days, you'll be able to adapt quickly and have many variants to test and prove. As you move through more and more teams, having multiple options on the go will put users into different methods, techniques and potentially solutions. Conflicting approaches could arise. In the longer term, this will make it much harder to scale and you could have data knowledge in different forms that will be hard to merge into a scalable solution and method. When the solution develops, converge on a single solution and get behind it so it can be the scaled solution for the organisation.

The end goal embedded will be continuous improvement.

VISION

Setting out the long-term vision at an early stage demonstrates why finding and removing waste is so important. Emphasise the scale of the problem to the organisation, which is typically 50% of capacity lost to waste. You need to show that removing waste will not only increase capacity to deliver more valuable products to customers but will also increase morale and make it a better place to work. The vision should illustrate the increased speed to market of products to customers via the reduction of waste and increased capacity to deliver more for the same cost.

Over time, this can become an integral part of the organisation's continuous improvement and organisational design toolkit.

TEAMWORK

Finding and removing waste is a team sport. Everyone in the organisation, from top to bottom and side to side, needs to buy into the idea and believe it will make a difference to them as individuals and the organisation as a whole.

DIRECTION

How do you keep your ideas on track and moving in the right direction? It starts with understanding who can help you on your journey and who might hinder. In any organisation you'll encounter different types of people who you can roughly categorise, as strategic thinkers, feelers, reflectors, those who are action-based, and so on.

Being aware of, and knowing how to spot, personality types can help. There are several common personality classification systems, including Myers-Briggs and the *16 Personality Types* in the book of that name by Dr A.J. Drenth. If you have been coaching for a while, your in-built personality radar will help you choose those who are capable of supporting the direction of travel at the appropriate time.

STRATEGY

Making the finding and removal of waste part of the organisation's long-term transformational strategy is essential for success. However, this can be an incredibly difficult part of the journey as your goal isn't established in reporting lines to the CEO's and various boards and director levels.

Nonetheless, it's important to back yourself because finding and removing waste is worth the prize. The work you are doing on storytelling, being available, and staying on message will be landing even when you cannot see the results.

The strategic level works at a glacial pace, though. In larger organisations, it can be a minefield to walk through, given the number of consultants in the mix trying to whip the cheese off the mouse trap. It could hold up your journey.

This is where language and tone are so important. Be in full-on sales mode and flip the solution. Instead of resolving waste that is sapping capacity and potentially costing millions every year, make it an opportunity. Tell them that under your leadership, they can help the organisation deliver great things with extra capacity.

When you talk to people, put yourself in their shoes. To go along with it, they'll need confidence in you personally, and what the vision and goal can achieve.

COMMUNICATION

Communication with the whole organisation should employ appropriate language. An easy way to think about language is to Use Customers'

Own Words (UCOW). In other words, what resonates with the problems they are trying to solve?

Hold community events, with story telling for all those areas involved such as but not including product owner, scrum master, business analysts, engineering communities and senior leaders.

The language for scrum masters may be waste (blockers) and knowledge to continually improve the performance of feature teams. But if you explain to a senior leader how wasteful their organisation is, you may not get the results you require. Instead of a senior leader, you could use the language, "We have an opportunity to use this method to increase capacity to deliver more products to customers at no additional cost. Are you interested?"

Also, allow those having success to tell the story, not just about success and how that felt but the journey they went on, both good and bad. The more authentic the experience, the better. We don't need to kid anyone, as we are here to make this a better organisation together. VLogs, podcasts, presentations, and Q&A sessions are all good for this. You just need to keep landing the message, even if it's just a 1:1.

GOAL

The goal is to remove waste at scale and reduce the 50-70% capacity that's being lost in the organisation. [1]

The goals are as follows:

1. Find Waste
2. Remove Waste
3. Increase capacity (which you do by removing waste)
4. Increase the speed of products to customers

---

[1] The Waste Detectives (Methods and Techniques)

By doing this, you will increase capacity and create a continual learning and improvement culture from top to bottom. This will improve the speed to market of products to customers and produce a better workplace for the transformational employees.

WHO YOU'LL NEED TO INFLUENCE

Let's look at the roles in the organisation you'll need to influence.

ROLE - CHANGE DIRECTOR

Description

Responsible for transformational change across the entire organisation. They could be responsible for tens or even thousands of colleagues and third-party supplier contracts. Change budgets can range from hundreds of thousands to billions for large organisations to keep delivering and adding new software products to be released to customers.

A Change Director is responsible for delivering as much meaningful product to customers as possible, this will be constrained by the amount of capacity available to maintain the flow of work to customers. The capacity available to a Change Director throughout the Teams, Labs and Value Streams can be increased by removing waste that saps that capacity in the Teams and Labs, This intern will make the organisation more competitive.

Why influence?

In order to roll out, senior leaders in the organisation are going to need encouragement.

The change director helps bring those who report into them on the journey by selling the **vision / goal / strategy** to the organisation.

ROLE - AGILE COACHES

Description

As the CTO's role being in charge of the organisation's computer systems, technology and processes that deliver products and services to customers, removing waste and increasing capacity helps deliver more to the customers for less cost, the CTO can bring in agile coaches to change mindsets and behaviours.

These agile coaches can have difficult conversations with leaders, product owners, and scrum masters.

The persons in an organisation would probably have some ingrained behaviours but without being open to change, it could make it incredibly difficult to change how the persons within the organisation feel about finding and removing waste.

Why influence?

Agile coaches can help sell the **vision / communication**. They can work with the organisation and you to find and remove waste.

ROLE - PRODUCT OWNERS

Description

Product owners are driven to want their meaningful product in the customer's hands as quickly as possible to provide a fast feedback loop.

You can find out more about product owners in Geoff Watts' book, *Product Mastery*.

Why influence?

Product Owners know how much capacity is being sapped by using the techniques mentioned earlier. They will hopefully want to learn how their team or labs works in order to understand how waste impacts the flow of products to customers.

Scaling the solution is essential to having their teams / lab and tribes deliver as much value as possible.

They will help with the **communication / vision** to scale the process.

ROLE - SCRUM MASTERS

Description

scrum masters coach on agile methods and work mainly at a team level in organisations. They are an essential resource in building agile capacity in teams.

Having Scrum Masters understand the flow and impact of waste on a team and organisation helps remove it. Effectively, this is the basic building block of how you scale capability throughout the organisation.

Why influence?

Scrum Masters will help sell the **vision**, deploy the **solution** on the ground, and test and learn in a number of areas.

They will provide feedback as to whether the method is working or if you need to adapt or tweak working practices to help remove waste at scale.

ROLE - BUSINESS MANAGEMENT

Description

Business management, sometimes referred to as the Programme Management Office (PMO), maintains the governance, risks and budgeting of an area.

It's essential to have business management with you on the journey towards understanding capacity, funding models and the flow of products to customers. They may have to move from the traditional to the adaptive world, so they'll need to know how capacity can be measured and reported and how finding and removing waste can improve capacity.

Why influence?

Business management will help with the **communication** towards the goal.

At times, you can expect business management to be asked to pull information together for leaders. Some of this information will relate to finding and removing waste and capacity metrics. They can also help with guidance and control through effective policies across a number of product owners to ensure a consistent message in the future.

Influencing Techniques

Now let's look at some of the things to consider when moving towards your goal of finding and removing waste from an organisation. Remember that you are trying to reduce the circle of concern and increase your circle of influence.

What does it take to become an influencer? In his book *The Art of Influencing People*, George Green explains that influencers:

1. Have an eye for the future
2. Are fearless
3. Are patient
4. Are big on experiments
5. Are relatable
6. Are creative
7. Hold unshakable main values
8. Are thoroughly consistent
9. Know how to handle criticism
10. Have a sense of humour

As a CTO, you've got point 1 covered. But what about the rest? Let's look at those other traits and see how they fit into the mission of finding and removing waste.

The following traits you'll need as CTO, but also those who are embedding The Waste Detectives Methods capabilities who are aiding the delivery of The Waste Detectives Methods approach, those could include agile coaches and scrum masters.

You need to **be <u>fearless</u>** at the outset if you want to start removing waste at scale. The data and size of the problem will shock you and senior leaders can't or won't want to believe it. However, with over 50% of capacity being drained from organisational capacity, it is no laughing matter. You just need to be confident and show that you believe in it when you stand before them. This isn't easy. When I first developed *The Waste Detectives*' methods and techniques and proved that they could successfully remove waste, one of my closest friends urged me to back myself. If I wasn't confident, it would show when I presented to potential clients and leaders. I had coaching to help me become more fearless. You'll need to find a way that works for you.

Building up your data and proving the method within the organisation will take time and you'll need to be **<u>patient</u>**. It could be a case of one team at a time before it starts to scale to many teams expanding the method via multiple teams at the same time. You will be chomping at the bit to progress, but you'll have to wait for a good set of waste data. When scrum masters see a good set of waste data, it gives them knowledge about what is slowing them up. They are able to act on it to remove impediments. At this point, leverage the scrum master community if one is established and, if not, create one. Get those peer-to-peer scrum master conversations going to increase the awareness of The Waste Detectives Methods throughout the scrum master communities, this will grow your level of influence as a CTO.

Note: Not all scrum masters will be keen. Recall Tony and his reluctance to buy jeans online. You will encounter scrum masters who don't want to try something new. This has always baffled me as scrum masters are there to increase capability and method, to help those persons in a team to have the capability to use methods such as the waste detectives. But go with those who are interested and don't have your energy sapped by the Tonys of this world. They will come around eventually; they just need more time and awareness to join you on the journey.

The scrum masters can then layer in the concept to the product owners, team by team initially, then gradually growing into a lab and then many labs. The product owners may also be wary, so **patience** is needed. But once they can see the delay and capacity being sapped from what they can deliver to customers as meaningful products, you'll slowly encourage individuals to get onboard. This is how you'll first convince a team, then many teams and labs, and eventually all or most of the organisation.

You'll need more **patience** dealing with those higher up. The higher up you go, the slower and longer influencing takes. In agile transformations, spinning up teams and labs to add capability and willingness in scrum or kanban is relatively quick. Layering in the finding and removing of waste is also quick – anything from a few months up to 24 months depending on the size and structure of the organisation. The teams and labs want to embrace change and execs at the top want the business to be more adaptive and increase capacity. But those in senior leadership roles are resistant. Some refer to this as the frozen middle. The more senior the person, the more ingrained their behaviours and unwillingness to adapt and consider new ideas. It could be because they are nearing retirement, it could be a loss of power, or perhaps they are fearful of change and what it means to them personally. Whatever the reason, it's a slow burn and it's about trying different languages and styles to see if the organisation is willing and wants to improve and become more adaptive.

Empowering teams by helping them use their own data, rather than see it as yours or Business Management's, allows them to start to build **experiments** and **creativity**. Cross-sharing these ideas across the organisation with media channels and podcasts will widen your reach throughout the organisation and make others curious. This is good but it can also cause problems. The more people involved, the more others will try to pull your work in other directions. **Hold to your unshakable main values** and stick to the goal of finding and removing waste and be **thoroughly consistent**. Experiments will provide knowledge and show you what is working and not working via scientific methods, and you can use the knowledge to drive change.

But several experiments can provide several solutions. To scale, you will need to lead and potentially choose a single direction at some stage. Leading the way, you are effectively working as a product owner tasked with finding and removing waste. In the long term, ideally a single method will drive economies of scale by collecting and acting on waste knowledge.

The more people in the organisation you reach, the more you'll open yourself up to **criticism**. This is normal. There are people you can influence and those who bite back at the ideas. Remember Tony, who was never going to buy jeans over the internet? I wonder if he shops online in 2023.

As an example from my own career, here is some of the **criticism** directed at me when I was developing the methods and techniques outlined in Waste Detectives Methods:

- "I have done this before and this isn't new." – this was a strange comment because it was indeed new and was later rolled out

to the entire organisation. I perceived this person as a career climber, ignored the comment and carried on.
- "This technically isn't right." – this comment went out to a large number of individuals in a group chat, in capital letters no less! Following the session, I spoke to two peers of the commenter. One said I should work with them and the other told me to ignore them because they'd sap my energy. I tried both, and ignoring them proved more productive for the concept and the organisation.
- "You shouldn't have done it like this, but like this." – If I had a pound for every time I heard this, I'd be Warren Buffett! This comes back to you acting as a design authority on finding and removing waste. With large transformations, there are always many ways to do things. But if you do all of them, you'll either never finish or you'll have unaligned data with no common goal. This comes down to backing yourself and making decisions on the most appropriate way forward at the time. Sometimes you may need a tactical way forward, before acting more strategically later on.

Negative comments will occasionally arrive, as the examples above show. But the amount of support and goodwill will grow too, as ultimately you are trying to make the organisation a better place by finding and removing friction and pain points that sap capacity and lower morale.

A good technique I was once told when negative criticism arrives is to kill the person in kindness and shower them in love. I would tell someone I loved their comments and that I would take them away, consider and reflect on them. Some, of course, may be valid whilst others might go straight in the bin.

The CTO and those working for the CTO embedding the methods such as agile coaches and scrum masters will need **unshakable** values.

To be truly effective, this needs to be someone's sole role and the organisation should back the work in terms of its value and importance.

My recommendation to you as the CTO is to resource fully and allow them to work as a mix of product owner and sole design authority.

The risk of not having a sole product owner / design authority is that you could struggle to contain a strategic scalable solution. You could end up with lots of different methods that fail to deliver a waste knowledge repository, which we will explore later. The reason for this is that as you scale, there will be many that will throw **criticism** at both you and the concept of finding and removing waste. Many hundreds of people and roles will want it delivered a different way. Make sure you listen to, and acknowledge, their ideas as there will be some good ones to progress and consider.

You'll hear some views that go against the long-term vision and strategy. scrum masters and agile coaches will potentially have a local solution, but if you said yes to all the local solutions, you would never have consistent knowledge in order to act on and make decisions based on the waste data. As a leader of the removing waste at scale, it is for you to make a decision. Then advise those with the local solutions of those other options by saying "No and "Why not".

Getting used to saying "No" to people, and explaining why, is something I struggled with initially. But in order to scale a concept across a large transformation programme, there are core ways of working that will need to be embedded. Take the lead and stick to your **unshakable** values.

Suggested Reading - George Green, (2021), The Art of Influencing People[2].

All of this can test your resolve, so try and keep a **sense of humour**. Think of all the presentations and talks you've seen. The ones you remember are probably those that had an element of humour. Knowing this will help those you interact with scrum masters, product owners, third parties, change directors, agile coaches, and business management. You obviously want them to think of you when they ask themselves, "Who was that who came to talk to us about finding and removing waste?"

---

[2]   Suggested Reading - George Green, (2021), The Art of Influencing People

An example of this is when I was working with a product owner called Nia and a colleague named Rob. Having already done some preparatory work in Nia's area, I knew that the amount of waste we were about to expose would be shocking. I decided that the best approach would be to soften the mood by injecting some humour.

Rob explained that, perhaps he should be referred to as "Dyno-Rod" this relates to a UK company who deals with blocked drains, where smelly waste needs to be removed, not the type of waste we are referring to here. But we all chuckled and "Dyno-Rod" stuck.

Rob explained to Nia that whilst no one wants to be told how ugly their baby is, the reality of the situation wasn't just bad for her but for everyone. In all the calls after that to discuss the fix, someone said, "Dyno-Rod, how are you going to help us remove waste?" This made it a team effort and something we could laugh about whilst resolving some of the big blockages in the system of change led by Nia.

However, remember the manager from *The Office*? The humour needs to be appropriate and, unlike David Brent, you should sound out the audience first. As I did with Rob when i explained if he was OK with the nickname,

COMMON LEADERSHIP CHALLENGE - SCENARIO (WASTE FOUND)

I once worked with a mid-level leader, who we'll call Sally. Sally was a product owner and realised that the lab and team structure had ineffective hands-offs in the Kanban system they were operating. Sally set out to gather data on the number of days being lost in terms of speed to market of product and the number of waiting days in terms of waste.

With this knowledge of the problem, Sally was able to make an intervention in the lab and team structure. By aligning the resource to the team, Sally prevented the dependency that was causing waste in the system. From being in the work and having learned about the issue for herself, this leader had seen the benefit. If we relate this example back to Tony, Sally would be the one buying the jeans online with no fear.

A while later, we were looking to embed and roll out these methods across the organisation. The waste methods have proven their worth: waste was being found and removed and capacity was increasing. Now, leaders were needed to roll it out.

In a meeting with a senior leader we'll call Nigel, Sally and I explained the concept of valuable work being stopped in the workflow and not being able to progress. (*This is the value that Nigel wants delivered*). The work could not progress for a period of days, in some cases many days. And yet the fact that value was not being delivered to customers met with not even a flicker of concern.

"I assume they can work on other work items?" asked Nigel.

The answer, of course, was yes. But the value work he wanted could not be progressed. So they were keeping themselves busy with non-valuable or less valuable work. This is a behaviour you will encounter amongst traditional leaders, as I have many times.

Of course, traditional methods such as waterfall can be comfortable if people are busy, even though valuable meaningful products are not flowing to customers. But to be Waste Detectives and remove waste at scale, we need the work flowing and a predictable pace of delivery. Having it blocked saps the flow rates of meaningful products to customers.

Recommended Reading on Flow: Danial S. Vacanti, (2015), Actionable Agile Metrics for Predictability[3]

It boils down to this. Traditional leaders want to keep people busy, whilst adaptive digital minded leaders want to keep work busy (meaningful value products flowing to customers).

To explore why this happens, let's look at the concepts of resource efficiency and flow efficiency and play a little game.

---

[3] Danial S. Vacanti, (2015), Actionable Agile Metrics for Predictability

RESOURCE EFFICIENCY VERSUS FLOW EFFICIENCY

Resource Efficiency

The aim of resource efficiency is to try and keep all your resources busy, aiming to be as close to 100% utilised as possible.

Flow Efficiency

The aim of flow efficiency is to add value for the client and progress the item of value from the time it is identified to the time it is delivered and being used by the end customer. The aim is to reduce the time taken for work to flow to the customer and be as predictable as possible in moving, reducing the time taken to get the product into the customer's hands.

EXERCISE A - FLOW

One way to illustrate flow and work efficiency is the Coin Game. It is often used by agile coaches to illustrate the efficiency of the flow value work to customers. You'll find a good example on YouTube: https://www.youtube.com/watch?v=fh4nkQnWL6I[4]

The game involves four people who need to pass coins to each other in batches. Each person has to turn the coin over.

The aim is to get the work flowing as efficiently as possible. At the start, you will recognise the case where management aims to keep all the resources (people) fully utilised. The players come to realise over a number of rounds (up to five) how the work and value can be achieved more efficiently.

---

[4]   https://www.youtube.com/watch?v=fh4nkQnWL6I

Prerequisites:

- Bag of coins
- Stopwatch
- Pen
- Paper
- Team of four people (employees)

Round 1

- The Team has 20 coins and all 20 coins need to be turned over by colleague 1 before they are passed to colleague 2.
- Colleague 2 then turns all the 20 coins over again until they are passed to colleague 3.
- Colleague 3 then turns all the 20 coins over again until they are passed to colleague 4.
- Colleague 4 then turns all the 20 coins over again.

Time how long it takes to get all 20 coins turned over from the start at colleague 1 through to the end at colleague 4.

Round 2

- The Team has 20 coins in two batches of 10 coins. When colleague 1 has turned over the whole batch of 10 coins, they can be passed to colleague 2 to start.
    - Colleague 1 completes the second batch of 10 coins, then passes them to colleague 2.
- Colleague 2 then turns over the first batch of 10 coins, then passes them to colleague 3 to start.

- o Colleague 2 completes the second batch of coins then passes them to colleague 3.
- Colleague 3 then turns over the first batch of 10 coins before passing them to colleague 4 to start.
  - o Colleague 3 completes the second batch of coins then passes them to colleague 4.
- Colleague 4 then turns over the first batch of 10 coins and then does the same with the second batch of 10 coins.

Time how long it takes to get all 20 coins turned over from the start at colleague 1 through to the end at colleague 4.

Round 3

- The Team has 20 coins and when the colleague has turned over the first batch of 5 coins, they can be passed to colleague 2 to start. Colleague 1 completes the second batch of 5 coins and passes them to colleague 2.
  - o Colleague 1 completes the second batch of 5 coins, then passes them to colleague 2.
  - o Colleague 1 completes the third batch of 5 coins, then passes them to colleague 2.
  - o Colleague 1 completes the fourth batch of 5 coins, then passes them to colleague 2.
- Colleague 2 then turns over the first batch of 5 coins and passes them to colleague 3 to start.
  - o Colleague 2 completes the second batch of coins then passes them to colleague 3.
  - o Colleague 2 completes the third batch of 5 coins, then passes them to colleague 3.
  - o Colleague 2 completes the fourth batch of 5 coins, then passes them to colleague 3.

- Colleague 3 then turns over the first batch 5 coins then passes them to colleague 4 to start.
    - Colleague 3 completes the second batch of coins then passes them to colleague 4.
    - Colleague 3 completes the third batch of 5 coins, then passes them to colleague 4.
    - Colleague 3 completes the fourth batch of 5 coins, then passes them to colleague 4.
- Colleague 4 then turns over the first batch of 5 coins and then does the same with the second, third and fourth batches of 5 coins, until all are complete.

Time how long it takes to get all 20 coins turned over from the start at colleague 1 through to the end at colleague 4.

What happened?

Not surprisingly, round 2 will be quicker than round 1 because it takes less work-in-progress at any one round for each person. Round 3 should be the quickest due to the smaller size of the batch which can be finished more quickly, with work arriving with the customer at the quickest pace. They start to get the first bit of work earlier, so you can get feedback earlier.

As an addition to the game, what if colleague 2 needs to take a call for a meeting? How would this waste (blockage) affect the flow rate of value work to the customer?

The Coin Game exercise is something your agile coaches can do with teams within your organisation.

By looking at your own work, when you have waste (blockers), ask yourself: is it better for my developer to be working on something that isn't important to the customer, just to keep busy? Or is it better that the work flows smoothly and is efficient in its progress to the customers?

It is about helping the teams to be more efficient and effective in the flow of products to customers. Finding and removing waste and making incremental, organisation-design changes allow the products to flow to customers in the most efficient way. Lose the obsession to keep everyone busy.

HOW A CTO CAN USE THESE TECHNIQUES

Set your strategy to continuously improve the organisation to increase the pace of delivery.

Explain the journey to your senior leaders the need for senior leaders to be more adaptive digital leaders. Scaling the waste methods is an opportunity for all those in the organisation to have an agreed shared purpose on how the organisation will have more efficiency in their delivery of product to customers. Helping make the organisation as efficient and effective as possible in delivery of products to customers.

Build a group of individuals around you to aid the influencing such as agile coaches of The Waste Detectives Methods throughout the organisation, and support them. These individuals helping you influence will have their resilience tested. Put in place training and coaching to help rebuild up the resilience when needed.

It is important to remember not everyone is going to be ready to want to scale The Waste Detectives Methods, remember Tony.

PRACTICAL STORY

Personally my scaling of The Waste Detectives Methods in an organisation, tested my resilience to the limits, but was fortunate enough to have some great support around me. What amazed me was the number of individuals who got the concept very quickly at a team and then into a lab level and could make a real difference to how people felt in a team and lab. This made individuals in the teams feel better, waste was reduced and flow increased.

Removing waste also increased our ability to embed 'test and learn' approaches, as the delays in the previous ways of working, meant we didn't have time to test new products prior to implementation.

When scaling up however, I met stiffer resistance and individuals with strong characters very quick to dismiss the concepts without having even tried the method. I find this similar to persons who order food in a restaurant and then sprinkle salt on to the food without having a taste first.

But now having gone through the influencing journey and enabled The Waste Detectives Methods to scale, it was a very rewarding journey to scale The Waste Detectives Methods Even those who were unwilling to support at first, found it hard to ignore when they saw the benefits being realised by those who had embraced The Waste Detectives Methods.

SUMMARY

This is going to be a long journey. At all stages, look for the opportunity to grow your circle of influence and empower those around you with the same values and core beliefs in your vision and goal. Bring in ideas from scrum masters and product owners, among others, and build on them. As a CTO, your circle of influence is limited. You are going to have to get more and more people to buy into your vision of finding and removing waste.

As this community grows, your task becomes one of encouraging and backing these individuals to go after the vision and be fearless. At the same time, you should lead and coordinate work towards the vision, acting in the role of a product owner for waste reduction yourself. Smile, support, and encourage all those who want to help the vision land.

Own the concept of finding and removing waste and be fearless. Have a tough outer shell to deflect criticism and smile along the way. Above all, enjoy it!

Over time, it is amazing to see something that you have nurtured and supported flourishing across the organisation. You'll feel pride in how this has made a real difference to the organisation and all those who work within it.

TAKEAWAYS

- ⇨ Always maintain direction towards your goal / vision.
- ⇨ Manage your circle of influence.
- ⇨ Manage your circle of concern and listen
- ⇨ It will take time for the vision to be adopted.
- ⇨ Not everyone can be influenced – remember Tony and his jeans.
- ⇨ Stay positive and believe in the product; it's a long journey.
- ⇨ Patience is essential.
- ⇨ Enjoy it.

CHAPTER 2
BEHAVIOURS OF DIGITAL LEADERS IN THE WORK

As a **CTO**, SETTING THE TONE and style of leadership behaviours provides hope to the senior leaders of value streams, labs and platforms. To quote a famous leader "A leader is a dealer of hope" (Napoleon Bonaparte, 1769-1821). In your role, this is also true. You are hoping for continuous improvements and the removal of waste in the organisation to make it as competitive as it can be in delivering meaningful products to customers.

In order to increase your hopes of success, the behaviour of the senior leaders and their reports into labs and teams need to carry the hope and also want to learn and adapt to allow the organisation to be more successful and remove waste and be more competitive. An area that can reduce hope, in the teams and throughout the organisation is to have senior leaders with a traditional mindset, in this chapter we will explore what is a senior leader with a traditional mindset versus an alternative digital mindset. Then look at some ways on how you can start the journey of working with your senior leaders to help them transition from traditional to an alternative mindset.

The power of real change comes from the human interaction and energy (Thomas 2019)

KEY CONCEPTS

Many organisations are now realising that their leaders need to maximise the use of technology to deliver meaningful products to customers. How organisations, leaders, teams and labs exploit these technologies will determine the winners and losers among businesses that are transforming to a digital world.

Leaders need to relish the opportunity and innovate, adapt and experiment to deliver regular delivery of new code / products to the customers. They need to be able to measure if the new code and products and services are wanted by the customer and can also generate revenue for the organisations.

Leaders need to have a defined purpose for the products they are trying to deliver to customers, and should ideally have a growth mindset.

Figure 2.1 : Digital Leader
Image by Andrey_Popov / Shutterstock.com

The digital leader's role is to deliver valuable consumable products to customers at pace and understand customer trends. They need to be able to adapt, or even stop, product production to pivot into a new product line that delivers value and what matters to the customer.

The need and demand for digital minded leaders has skyrocketed since the Covid-19 pandemic as most companies realise that the move to digital products and services is only going to increase in future.

This journey requires digital leaders, but these leaders are few in number and in great demand. Many traditional organisations have a problem here, as their leaders are from a project management/programme management background. Often, the directors of these organisations also come from a project/programme-management background. They are traditional leaders with command and control behaviours, which is totally different to what's needed for the future.

Those who have been successful in the past, in a traditional working environment, may not have the mindset at the moment to be adaptive leaders for the future.

"Zero In On Your Pain Points"

Quote from *The Digital Leader: Finding Faster More Profitable Path To Exceptional Growth*, Ram Charan and Raj Vattikuti

Digital minded leaders need to maximise the technology but, as they are transforming and delivering, they will encounter pain and friction points in terms of how the organisation is set up and currently operates. We touched on organisation design earlier, and it's described in more detail in *Team Topologies* by Mathew Skelton and Manuel Pais. In order to find interaction and pain points to remove waste, The Waste Detectives Methods emerged.

When I produced The Waste Detectives Methods, I was lucky to work with a leader I named Graham in the book (*The Waste Detectives Methods and Techniques*). Graham understood the need for the right behaviours of encouragement and collaboration and began in the work to gain knowledge to act on the system.

Graham held sessions with his direct reports and then introduced sessions with the scrum masters to demonstrate the waste in the lab, in order to assist them in the removal of the waste, this allowed areas to deliver faster and have more capacity.

Digital minded leaders with the right mindset will want to churn through the waste knowledge they are finding in order to act. They'll want to remove interaction pain points and get the most from the technology to deliver meaningful products at pace for customers.

TRADITIONAL VERSUS ADAPTIVE (DIGITAL LEADERS)

As a CTO, you'll want adaptive digital minded leaders rather than traditional ones. Let's have a brief look at the two leadership philosophies and look at where they came from.

In the early 1900s, Henry Ford was setting up his motor car factory and needed management and leadership to enable it to function. As he was an early pioneer of mass production, he needed leadership philosophy so he engaged the services of Frederick Winslow Taylor. Taylor advised Ford to have specialist teams responsible in functional, top-down specialist areas, driven by targets and keeping people busy. It's still used in many thousands of organisations to this day with programme managers and project managers but the concept is now over 100 years old.[5] I will refer to this philosophy as the traditional paradigm.

Having looked at Henry Ford, now let's look at Japan after the second world war.

After the Second World War, Japan needed to be rebuilt from devastation. Toyota called on William Edwards Deming to bring in a management philosophy which is referred to as the Deming Wheel - Plan Do Check Act (PCDA). The focus was continuous improvement and making the workplace more efficient and successful. It was formed

---

[5] https://nanoglobals.com/glossary/scientific-management-theory-of-frederick-taylor/

around the core of understanding customers' and colleagues' needs, improving processes and eliminating waste. It makes me wonder if W.E. Deming would have signed up to become a waste detective! [6]

In the table below, we are now going to look at different perspectives related to traditional ways of working versus alternative (digital) ways of working.

Leadership Capabilities	Traditional (Ways of Working)	Alternative (Digital)
PERSPECTIVE	Top-Down functional specialisation	Outside in
BASIS FOR ACTION	Experience	Knowledge (data)
DECISION MAKING	Separated from work	Integrated in work
MOTIVATION	Extrinsic	Related to purpose
MEASURES	Budget, targets, outputs, standards	Intrinsic (self motivated)
MANAGEMENT & ETHICS	Budgets and people	Act on the value stream, lab (system)
ATTITUDE TO CUSTOMERS	Contracts	What matters for the customer

Figure 1.2 : Traditional versus Alternative (Digital) Leadership
(from Freedom from Command and Control, John Seddon)

PERSPECTIVE

In the traditional ways of working, organisations and leaders are typically set up in functional specialisms. In the Change world, this could be business analysis, business architects, testers, etc. Who all work within their specialist fields only . In the digital world of change, we tend to look at the work from outside in. Teams are set up that relate to a particular feature or product, with relative skills and capability within the

---

[6] https://deming.org/

team to deliver. This might be a cross blend of skills where analysis does testing and testing does analysis. The team and leaders are all connected to the same piece of work for the customer outcomes.

Having functional specialisms causes hand-offs, and this causes delay and waste in your system of change. To find and remove this waste, leaders can break down these functional specialisms to improve the flow of work.

BASIS FOR ACTION

In the traditional ways of working, leaders from specialist fields tend to get promoted and act on their past experiences. But at this stage, leaders are distant from the work and the value of that experience is worth less and less to the organisation. The adaptive (digital) leader is in the work. They act on the knowledge and the data showing what is working, what the customer of the products wants and what is slowing them down.

DECISION MAKING

In the traditional ways of working, leaders are separated from the work. Consider a traditional leader such as a project manager or programme manager who is separated from the work, creating project plans and programme plans but not actually connected to the people doing the work or the problem being solved for customers. They're making decisions based on their experience from a while ago and plans that aren't connected to the work for the customer. They are more like contractual agreements to deliver something on a set date.

In contrast, digital (adaptive) leaders are connected to the purpose and outcome of what the value stream, lab or teams are trying to deliver for the customer. Leaders know the purpose, pace and flow of the work towards producing the outcome. They know what is slowing the work down.

MOTIVATION

In the traditional ways of working, organisations could have balance score card models whereby 5% of employees and/or department leaders get no pay rise. The next 25% get a very low pay rise, 40% an average award and 25% a slightly better one. The top 5% get a large pay rise.

Let's look at the behaviours that this could drive within a traditional leadership setup. If a leader was in line for a huge pay rise and a peer was also close to that level, would those leaders help each other or work against each other?

In the adaptive (digital) leadership setup and mindset, the leader and organisation are purpose-driven towards adding value for the customers. The dog eat dog culture of the balanced scorecard does not exist.

MEASURES

In traditional ways of working, organisations typically measure budgets, targets, outputs, and standards. They are focused on measuring the plan and the budget being spent. A useful technique as a change consultant is to ask leaders to show you how they are delivering value products to the customers. Sometimes you will only get back the budget, targets, outputs, standards and timesheets. When you ask how much value you have delivered to the customer, you may get a blank response.

The adaptive (digital) leader will want to measure the flow and value release of the work being delivered to customers related to the purpose or the outcome. Hopefully they'll also want to know what is slowing the pace of value products to customers in the form of waste.

MANAGEMENT AND ETHICS

In the traditional ways of working, leaders tend to be interested in people and budgets. It is more important to keep people busy rather than keeping the work busy.

ATTITUDE TO CUSTOMERS

In the traditional ways of working, leaders tend to have a contractual focus. They agree on a plan and deliverables, whilst an adaptive (digital) leader is focused on what matters to the customer.

Let's explore the above and how it looks and sounds in practice. Today, 70 years from Japan and Deming, we are in the digital age. The need to have adaptive digital minded leaders is now incredibly important to organisations, so why has leadership not moved with the times?

Figure 2.3 : Digital Leader
Image by Matej Kastelic / Shutterstock.com

These changes can take a long time. The Singapore-based DBS group was transformed by CEO Piyush Gupta, starting in 2009. Now the bank has been named the "World's Best Digital Bank" twice by *Global Finance Magazine*. Its chief technology officer Paul Cobban talks about how the DBS used to be called "Damn Bloody Slow" prior to its transformation to becoming the World's Best Bank. [7]

Cobban has said that discovering the sheer scale of waste within DBS was a wake-up call. Once they understood the scale of the problem, it was then about getting decision-makers to drive innovation. This is where The Waste Detectives Methods and this book can help you. [8]

Transforming from a traditional bank or another kind of legacy organisation is achievable if you have the right leaders and mindset.

DIGITAL LEADER CHARACTERISTICS

Let's have a look at some of the key leadership characteristics, using Elon Musk as an example.

Vision Shaping

Twitter, Inc's vision is to give everyone the power to create and share ideas and information instantly without barriers.

Think Beyond Boundaries

Elon clearly has a plan to go beyond how Twitter was operating before he purchased the company. Only time will tell what that plan is and whether it has worked.

---

[7] https://www.cuscalpayments.com.au/news/videos/dbs-incredible-digital-transformation-with-paul-cobban/

[8] The Digital Leader Finding Faster More Profitable Path To Exceptional Growth, Ram Charan and Raj B. Vattikuti (2022) Pages 21 - 25

Curiosity

He is curious and wants to know about what the customer wants through data and leverages technology to make things happen.

Collaborate and deliver in adversity

We can only surmise that Elon Musk's network of contacts is massive and he delivers in adversity. He built the Tesla electric car company and put a rocket in space (which also launched a Tesla into orbit). We can only wait and watch to see what happens to Twitter.

Experiment

Experimentation is the nature of how Elon operates. He's always trying new things and the companies he runs follow the same ethos.

Take Risks

There is no doubt that Elon is a risk taker. But he has been successful in the past through taking risks and his ability to adapt.

Network

We can only assume that Elon has a huge number of contacts he can draw upon and utilise.

TRADITIONAL LEADER BEHAVIOURS

Non-digital minded leaders from project and programme management backgrounds tend to have command and control characteristics that are not well suited to the digital age of transformation. Let's have a brief look at why this may not be useful to your journey.

Vision Shaping

These leaders want to keep resources busy and generally track to a milestone plan. They can have no alignment to the outcome that the vision is looking to achieve because they are typically head-down in delivery mode. They are focused on dates, targets, and what is in the contact and don't consider what is important to the customer.

Think Beyond Boundaries

They are unable to change how they operate, with a project or programme-management mindset and behaviours. Their decision making can be based on previous experience, which can be as useful as a plane with no wings.

These leaders' thinking can be based on the project plan or programme-management techniques of slowly building a plan. Once in place, they manage resources, budgets and risks to tick items off the list and hold to the plan. It demonstrates a lack of adaptability and a willingness to think outside of fixed boundaries.

Data, new technology and what is happening outside of their own area. Just managing the team to a plan will only get them what was in the plan on day 1.

Curiosity

Traditional leaders have a basis for action that typically comes from past experience. They are distant from work.

What happens when teams and labs discover that a large amount of waste is blocking them from delivering meaningful products at pace? With leaders who are distant from the work, teams and labs struggle to get those leaders into the work to create improvements by experiment.

I have seen this generate anger and frustration in the teams and it's a struggle to increase the pace of delivery. Anything you can do to get the leaders in the work is worthwhile.

Collaborate and deliver in adversity

Traditional leaders in some large organisations can work against each other. This can happen when the company motivates colleagues and leaders to set targets. This creates a dog eat dog, blame culture. Leaders manage the plan and don't allow resources to be used by other teams.

Experiment

They have no interest in experimenting or releasing delivery capacity to try something new. They just focus on delivering to the plan and what is contractually important.

Take Risks

No risks are taken. They are recorded and reported on for management information purposes.

Network

They have a limited network to do what they have done before. They have no hunger or have disincentives to increase knowledge or the capability to leverage others within the organisation and externally.

DIGITAL LEADER BEHAVIOURS

Vision Shaping

Have a view of the vision or purpose and focus on the making strives for archive the purpose is, only focused and curious on making directions towards that purpose, but possible with no fixed plan. The outcome is clear and owns the journey towards it, has defined the outcome and with others aligned the work and resources needed to achieve the outcome. The outcome has clear measurable points from a customer perspective to test and check if the outcome is progressing.

As the leader progresses toward the outcome, knowledge may determine a difference or adapted path for success. Let's look at this from the perspective of a very successful product led by digital leaders.

The digital minded leaders at Amazon created and launched the Fire Phone in 2104, expecting it to be a success and capture a good proportion of the smartphone market. It would have got them into some of the gap left by Nokia. The Amazon Fire Phone was an experiment backed by a lot of investment, but the product was rejected by its customers as the price was similar to the iPhone. Some of the people involved have said it felt like the team was building a phone for Bezos rather than something customers wanted. [9]

Not too surprisingly, the phone failed. Customers clearly didn't want the Fire Phone, but digital minded leaders in Amazon were hungry

---

[9]   https://www.productlessons.xyz/article/why-amazon-fire-phone-failed-case-study

for knowledge. They wanted to know what customers did like about the phone, if anything. It turned out that they liked being able to ask a question and get the answer from a piece of software called "Alexa". The leaders then took this knowledge, adapted the vision and backlog and tried again with an adjusted vision. Knowing what the customer wants, and where you can get value and demand, is what digital minded leaders are looking for, in their role as tech entrepreneurs. Fast forward to 2018 and Amazon sold 100 million Alexas in that year alone.

Think Beyond Boundaries

Now let's reflect on the Amazon Alexa Fire Phone. A traditional leader would have done a lessons-learnt exercise, maybe put them in a drawer and never looked at them again before moving on to the next project or programme. The digital minded leaders in Amazon, asked questions of what the customers like about the Amazon Fire Phone Failure, one common bit of knowledge they gleaned that customers liked asking the phone questions.

Now, I am sure it won't take three guesses as to what software feature customers liked in the Amazon Fire Phone. It was Alexa.

Let's bring back Elon Musk. He bought Twitter for $44 million. He has a vision that goes beyond its current boundaries to make it into a payments engine, something he wanted to do with PayPay 20 years ago. The long-term view is to allow Twitter users to have bank accounts on the app. He certainly thinks outside boundaries.

Curiosity

Digital minded leaders are curious about technology and what it can do for them. They want to know how they can deliver more meaningful products to customers and they think The Waste Detectives methods look like a good idea. They want to try it in their organisation's labs and teams to see if they can get increased capacity to deliver even more.

That ability to be curious drives the right attitude and a willingness to try new things and be brave. This can be infectious from the top down, throughout the organisation.

Collaborate and deliver in adversity

They are an equal, and not just someone who is managing a plan and thinking they are better than those in the work. They promote and live out the team concept of we are all in this together. They get into the work to understand what is slowing them down in terms of waste (blockers), as well as the success and great products that are being delivered to customers.

Experiment

They continually experiment with products going out to customers to understand the value it delivers back to the organisation. At the same time, they experiment in the work to remove waste and blockers, perhaps starting with one of the exercises in this book.

Take Risks

Using traditional ways of working, it takes a long time for customers to get products. Plus, there's a slow feedback loop in order to make improvements and adapt. But digital minded leaders have more of an ability to take risks, and taking risks generates rewards. You can take risks by getting products to customers as quickly as possible, measuring the usage, and listening to what customers are saying. By acting on knowledge and making things better for the customer, over time the risks will decrease. But in order to learn, you need to get something into customers' hands. Remember the Amazon Fire Phone? Amazon took a massive risk and it went wrong. But they tried again and that risk proved well worth taking in the long run.

So take risks to remove waste and try to deliver more products to your customer more quickly. If you change nothing, your delivery pace and capacity could remain the same. With The Waste Detectives Methods you can deliver more for less.

Network

Digital minded leaders are hungry to learn and get more and more knowledge to act on. This can include agile chat rooms, conferences, internal company presentations, and visiting other labs and companies to see what is working and not working. Then they have the ability to act on the knowledge over time to improve as a digital leader.

SO WHAT DOES THIS HAVE TO DO WITH FINDING AND REMOVING WASTE?

To act on knowledge to improve teams and labs, here as a CTO you will want digital minded leaders who think outside their current thinking parameters. To consider and try The Waste Detectives Methods, as described. They'll need the curiosity, mindset and self-belief to try something new. A good digital leader I once worked with was called a "data monster" by his teams and labs. They recognised his drive to work hard and gain knowledge about the way his change area operated. He had a desire to experiment, measure the results, and sense and act on the data for continuous improvement. Most of all, this leader had a willingness to take risks.

If you don't change anything, the team or lab will operate exactly as it is doing now. Think of Elon Musk who goes all in. I'm not saying you need to take that level of risk. But if you have found interactions and pain in your team or lab via The Waste Detectives Methods, it's worth making an intervention in how your team or lab is operating.

BUSINESS VALUE DELIVERED

Digital business leaders are hungry to search for, and measure, the business value being delivered to customers and clients. Some examples of this are:

- The speed of getting new products to market is faster (concept-to-launch date is quicker).
- Waste capacity is decreasing and value delivery capacity is increasing.
- Waste Detectives methods embedded.
- Performance time of customer transactions.
- Ability to scale across many millions of customers.
- Increased market share and improved base of customers.
- Optimised, faster, accurate solution.

EXERCISE

As a CTO, hold a session with your senior leaders and ask them a few questions in the room.

1. Explain the Traditional versus Alternative Paradigm shown in (Figure 7.2)
2. Draw up a rectangle on a wall or white board, traditional in the left box and alternative in the right box.

Traditional   **Adaptive**

3. Give them 7 Red Dots one for each perspective (Traditional)
   a) Top-Down functional specialisation
   b) Experience
   c) Separated from the work
   d) Extrinsic (Balance Score Card etc)
   e) Budget, targets, outputs, standards
   f) Budgets and people
   g) Contracts
4. Give them 7 Green Dots one for each perspective (Alternative)
   a) Outside in
   b) Knowledge (data)
   c) Integrated with the work
   d) Related to purpose
   e) Intrinsic (self motivated)
   f) Act on the value stream, lab (system)
   g) What matters for the customer
5. Ask them to mark up where they believe are today Traditional versus Alternative (Red Dot)
6. Ask them to mark up where they want to develop towards Traditional versus Alternative (Green Dot)
7. Ask them to choose which of the leadership capabilities they would like to improve in themselves.

The outcome of this exercise is that senior leaders choose the area in which they want to increase capabilities in becoming digital adaptive minded leaders.

Then from this, use CTO's delivery methods including The Waste Detectives Methods, and have your agile coaches running upskilling sessions with the leaders on this topic.

Were your senior leaders to choose wanting to develop areas such as Act on the value stream, lab (system), knowledge (data) and acting what is important to the customer. That would be a great opportunity to pull in the waste detectives method and have them more integrated with the work in teams collecting waste knowledge, with the leaders wanting to assist them and remove waste. A perfect opportunity to see how knowledge and acting on it as a senior leader can improve flow of products to customers and increase capacity.

Note: Repeat this session periodically to see how the capability is increasing.

PRACTICAL STORY

Working with a senior leader once, who was reluctant to try agile methods and move towards agile. The senior leader had a traditional programme that was failing to deliver. He reached out to me for suggestions and I recommended, kanban approach with limited work in progress and a heavy focus on finding and removing waste. The programme was turned around and delivered on time as well as what the customer wanted. This built up trust and credibility.

I used this to have an honest conversation on where things are moving commercially and how products are delivered via agile methods. Discussing where they are now and what it means for them in the longer term. Understanding the willingness to transition in the environment they are working in now. Generally this had a good take up and solid results in moving the mindset and behaviours from traditional leaders towards being adaptive digital leaders.

This proceeded agile coaching in a number of techniques including The Waste Detectives Methods, this senior leader has now transitioned from programme manager ways or working and has achieved a new role at the same level as a product owner.

I know moving from traditional to adaptive ways can be daunting, but with support and coaching this can enhance careers as well as pace of products being delivered to customers.

SUMMARY

In order to get senior leaders supporting and being in the work to help focus the organisation on wanting to improve and act on knowledge to remove waste and increase flow. There may be some work needed with senior leaders who may have many years of experience built up, delivering very well via traditional methods. However this would have built up behaviours that as a CTO you now want to unwind. So your leaders can act on knowledge such as waste information, to understand where the friction and pain points are in the organisation.

Having worked with a number of leaders on adaptive leadership, flow and the finding and removal of waste via experiments. When the senior leader lands the concepts, this is a powerful force that can energise a whole value stream. Then this happens. This is a joy to watch for all those in the value stream, as work flows and continuous improvements are on the forefront of everyone.

TAKEAWAYS

- Establish your leadership skill base and a willingness to change.
- Be clear on your goal and stay on message.
- Command and control leadership is not going to help you become a digital organisation.
- Coach the leaders and help them transition from an alternative minded leader into an adaptive leader.
- Digital minded leaders can aid you to remove waste and increase the capacity the organisation has to deliver value to customers.

CHAPTER 3
WASTE DETECTIVES' METHODS

THE WASTE DETECTIVES METHODS IS THE method as a CTO that you can scale across the organisation, to find knowledge (data) on the interactions and pain points that exist across value streams, labs and teams throughout the organisation. By understanding the methods and getting close to the waste knowledge, will help being able to influence across and down into organisations to help scale the method. Finding and removing waste is the cheapest way an organisation can improve pace of delivery, as it doesn't cost anything other than a change of mindset.

In this chapter, the book will cover the consequences of waste to the organisation and a series of proven Waste Detectives Methods and techniques to help find the waste within teams and labs. These can be used by the agile coaches and scrum masters in the organisation to embed the capabilities to find waste to expose interactions and pain points.

METHOD

The organisation that's engaged you is wasting at least 50%, possibly more, of its capacity.

For a company in the middle of a digital transformation journey, this is bad news. It needs to be adaptive to deliver meaningful products to customers as quickly as possible to maintain or grow market share. Waste isn't in the plan.

Once you start delving into measurements and risk records, you'll spot instances of technology not working or resources being unavailable or reassigned to more pressing demands. All of which causes delays that sap the organisation's capacity to deliver at pace, ultimately making it less competitive than its peers.

This is waste. Having waste in your organisation increases the work-in-progress (WIP) and adds to the amount of capacity that is being sapped from your transformation programme. In *The Art of Doing Twice the Work in Half the Time*, Jeff Sutherland estimates that up to 75% of capacity can be lost as a result.

In this chapter, we'll introduce methods you can use to identify waste. Specifically we'll look at:

- Understanding how to flag and capture waste data.
- Sensing the impact of waste on your organisation.
- Identifying the top blockers.

Let's start by looking at waste within teams and how to reveal it using the *Waste Detectives*' data capture techniques.

CAPTURING WASTE DATA WITHIN TEAMS

On identifying that a work item is blocked, create a ticket and capture four bits of information about the blockage:

- **Who** - Which team, lab or third-party organisation is blocking the work?
- **Why** - Why is work blocked?

- **Impact** - What is the impact of that piece of work being blocked? You may want to use a code to group the impacts, such as HH - High Impact - Hard to fix; HE - High Impact - Easy to Fix; LH - Low Impact - Hard to Fix; LE - Low Impact - Easy to Fix
- **Category** - Assign this type of blockage to a group of waste data.

A category is a theme or grouping of a collection of waste data knowledge types that you find, that you can roll up into a high level category grouping, as the examples listed below.

Examples could be as follows, but let your own data on waste lead you to your own categories.

- Within the Team.
- External to Team (with same company)
- 3rd Party Company
- Technical
- Governance

This will create a defined set of categories to help group the waste data into pots of the same categories (recommend only having a small group of between 5 and 9. Otherwise you'll collect more data than you can use.

Note : *There will be areas that want a massive list. Resist it!*

Having the category will allow you to pull these types of data and knowledge together more easily later, to be able to act on the information to make improvements.

This information can be captured manually or by using an agile tool. In Jira, for example, this information can be captured by right clicking on a work item such as an epic or user story, for example, and setting a flag with comments. This has the added benefit of automatically recording the blocked work start and end times, which can be used for knowledge. We will expand on this later on when we explore a waste knowledge repository.

Table 3.1. Example of how a team can capture waste data

WHO	ABC Company
WHY	The supplier has failed to supply company ABC for user story or task which is preventing Feature Team AAAA from delivering the AAAA Management Information (MI) report to Customer ABCD.
IMPACT	Customer ABCD needs this MI report in order to complete a report to the external regulator. Customer ABCD will not be able to trade and sell product AAAA until the MI report is received and signed off by the external regulator. HE - High Impact, Easy To Fix
CATEGORY	In the category of called "3rd Party Suppliers" of which there are many, such as • ABC Incorporated • XXX Limited • XYZ Systems The third party supplier named XYZ Systems is holding back work from progressing in a number of feature teams across a number of labs in the organisation preventing value work being delivered to customers.

Along with the information above, capture the following when work is blocked:

- **Blocked start date:** Date that the work item was blocked.
- **Blocked end date:** Date the work item was unblocked.

As your teams capture the data over a period of months, you'll be able to define and collaborate to build up the categories that would exist and work for you as a transformation in the organisation you are currently working, by feeling and sensing from "WHO" knowledge captured. The impacts might take longer than finding the problem and won't show you how hard it is to fix. So a description of the consequences to your organisation is a useful start. Over time, as you build up more and more knowledge, you'll be able to sense how easy or hard it is to fix the problems you are required to remove to allow work to flow freely.

EXERCISE: CAPTURING WASTE DATA WITHIN TEAMS

Go to your teams and ask them to comment on the causes of blocked work. Ask them to identify the most recently blocked work item using the template above. If the template isn't suitable for your organisation, change it and go again. Then you'll start to capture information that is slowing the flow of meaningful products to your organisation and is sapping capacity.

This will start to provide a set of knowledge of the type of pain and friction points that teams are facing when trying to deliver the products through the system of change to customers.

SENSING WASTE IN THE DATA CAPTURED

When considering waste, let's look at how this can impact the volume of waste data and how time lost to work being blocked can impact the organisation.

Capacity = Value Work + Waste

Capacity in the agile environment is the resource available in a team or lab process of work that is being used to deliver meaningful products to customers in the form of an outcome aligned to a purpose.

For example, a feature team in the lab delivers new payment functionality for a client on a smartphone, so they can pay with a new payment type. The development environment, testing, cloud storage and people are the capacity. These will be engaged in assembling the new software, are not active (waste), or are active on avoidable activity, such as resolving bugs from the software (also waste).

The more waste you can find and remove from the organisation, the more capacity you'll have to deliver more value work to your clients, making you more efficient and effective as a business.

From the perspective of an agile software development, the effective use of resources is clearly important and can be sensed through flow, particularly some of the flow metrics outlined by Mik Kersten in his book *Project to Product*:

- Flow Time.
- Flow velocity (Throughput).
- Flow efficiency.

Other metrics that help sense how well the resource is being used are:

- Number of defects.
- Amount of rejected work
- Amount of work-in-progress (WIP) that has been neglected.

Sensing and Insight

The core data items to gain knowledge of waste are:

Time (Duration) – The number of days that the work item has been held up (i.e. is waiting and cannot be progressed).

Who (Source) – Where in the organisation the source of the blockage originates; this could be a team, a department, a resource or even a role or capability.

What (Type) – A description of what is preventing the item or feature from progressing and therefore delaying its completion.

Impact (Effect) – Understanding the impact of an item or feature being held up is important to highlight the damage being done to performance, strategy, vision, and ultimately the organisation's survival. Build a 4-box table and use the codes of:

- HE - High Impact - Easy to Fix
- HH - High Impact - Hard to Fix
- LE - Low Easy - Easy to Fix
- LH - Low Impact - Hard to Fix.

Note: High Impact, Easy to Fix corresponds to the management phrase, "go after the low hanging fruit". In other words, these are the easy fixes that have a high impact on increasing the pace of flow of products to customers.

Category (Theme) – Grouped into the category names you have defined from the "WHO" knowledge collected as explained above.

This will allow you later to show the biggest problem is in terms of the quantity of waste. Note: This may not be the biggest impact, so sense your data and then decide where you want to perform an intervention.

EXERCISE: IDENTIFYING TOP BLOCKERS

Take the information your teams have been capturing (**Time (Duration)**, **Who (Source)**, **Category (Theme)**) and build a 2-bar chart:

- Show the Category of Waste by the number of days (capacity) lost.
- Show Who (Source) of Waste by the number of days (capacity) lost.

Question: How can you use this information?
Question: Is the organisation set up right or are there handoffs designed into the organisation that are not working?
Question: How are you going to act on the knowledge to make improvements?
Question: What changes are needed to improve the system of change?

GROUPING BY IMPACT

Take the information your teams have been capturing **Time (Duration)**, **Category (Theme)** for each item blocked and built and assigned to the chart below.

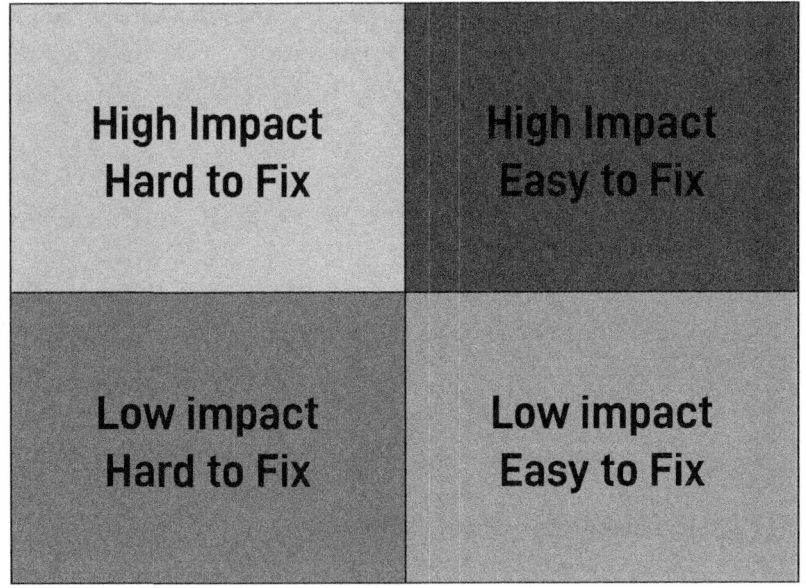

Table 3.2. Matrix table to visualise waste by Impact and Ease

Question: How can you use this information?
Question: Where is your most costly, easy-to-fix waste in your organisation?

Question: How are you going to act on the knowledge to make improvements?

EXERCISE

Having looked at the grouping data by impact, now have a look at some work that has been delayed by a number of days and by "WHO". Draw out the chart on a piece of paper like the one above and then go through the table below and write the Work ID and Time in days for each row as per the template above.

This exercise should show how the impact coding can help group the waste data / knowledge captured into a priority collection for fixing later within your system of change value stream, lab and team.

Table 3.3. Example of how a team can capture waste data

Work ID	Time (Duration of Delay)	Who (Source)	What (Type)	Impact (Effect)
Item0001	10 days	Database Development Team	External to Team (with same company)	Clients unable to buy products, the company cannot sell product X HE - High Impact - Easy to Fix
Item0002	05 days	Environment Support	External to Team (with same company)	The new version of software abc needs to be installed to ensure we remain on the newest version of software ABCD. LH - Low Impact - Hard to Fix.

Item0003	25 days	Governance meeting	Governance	The new code release has to be signed as secure by a governance committee. LE - Low Impact - Easy to Fix
Item0004	12 days	Database Development Team	External to Team (with same company)	Clients unable to buy products, the company cannot sell product X HH - High Impact - Hard to Fix
Item0005	2 days	Environment Support	External to Team (with same company)	The development team is able to release a new version of code, for security patch. HE - High Impact - Easy to Fix
Item0005	15 days	Release Team	Within the Team.	LE - Low Easy - Easy to Fix

You have a decision to make as you cannot solve all the waste and blockers. Which of the work items above do you prioritise to fix the blocker and release the work to complete for your customers?

Note : This table of waste information is a very small subset of what potentially could be hundreds if not thousands of rows of data. You may want to consider doing this exercise for each team, lab and roll up into a value stream. This would give you a useful mechanism to allow teams, labs and value streams to share insights into what is slowing down the release of value products to customers.

Value Stream -> Lab / Team

High Impact Hard to Fix	High Impact Easy to Fix
Low impact Hard to Fix	Low impact Easy to Fix

At this stage, use the data, collaborate, discuss, and have the team and lab workshops gain insight and then act on the most important waste in terms of blockers that are not only draining capacity but also slowing the flow of meaningful products to customers. It would offer a useful way to access the information via building automatically created reporting views of information using business rules.

Now we have covered grouping impacts of waste impact, let's now look at different types of waste.

TYPES OF WASTE

You can put in a framework to identify and study the seven different states of waste. This will give you visibility of three types of waste, an indication of two types, and knowledge of the consequences of two others.

The types of waste that are visible in an organisation if you know how to measure them are:

- Delays
- Partially done work
- Handoffs.

Two other types of waste can be identified from their indirect impact. These are:

- Task switching
- Relearning.

Figure 3.1. Seven waste types in software
Image by Olivier Le Moal / Shutterstock.com

The types of waste that are visible in an organisation if you know how to measure them are:

- Waiting (Delays)
- Partially done work (Overprocessing)
- Transportation (Handoffs)

Putting work down due to a handoff causes "task switching". Having to pick it back up again causes "relearning". Putting a task down and picking up another one increases work-in-progress (WIP). Research suggests that it takes 15 minutes to get up to speed to perform a task. Putting a task down and restarting it from scratch takes a further 25 minutes. This equates to 40 minutes each time it happens.

This may not seem like much. But if you scale it up across a large organisation, capacity and budgets are sapped by delays and wasted time and teams can get demotivated. In *The Art of Doing Twice the Work in Half the Time*, Jeff Sutherland estimates that up to 75% of capacity can be lost as a result.

Suggested reading Jill Duffy - [10]

So not only does having waste in your system of change team, lab or value stream slow the flow of meaningful products to customers, it also saps your organisation's capacity to deliver.

HOW A CTO CAN USE THESE TECHNIQUES

As CTO setting the vision to the value streams, labs and teams as a CTO is saying how important this is to yourself and the organisation and the need for information to act on in the form of knowledge waste (data). We discussed earlier how this can be supported and by senior leaders who are also on the journey to become more adaptive (digital) leaders.

---

[10] https://productivityreport.org/2016/02/22/how-much-time-do-we-lose-task-switching/

The agile coach and scrum masters will be your leverage, to embed the methods and capabilities to setting up conditions that may be safe for teams, labs and value streams to expose problems that exist in the organisation.

Then learn through experiments, which we will cover later in the book on how to make a change through continuous improvements to act on the waste found to remove it.

PRACTICAL STORY

On creating The Waste Detectives Methods, I learnt through experimentation at a team level then grew the methods upwards. Influencing at every stage to grow the capabilities into and upwards into the organisation which takes time. Trying to navigate a number of senior leaders along the way, sometimes successful and other times not.

The teams come up to speed finding and removing waste fairly quickly, then can establish this into their day to day working in the methods they are using such as scrum or kanban.

The advantage you have as a CTO is now the method is proven, the techniques work and this method can be a lift and drop of the techniques into any organisation.

SUMMARY

By having teams capture a relatively small amount of information, you can quickly sense and visualise where problems exist. Visualising and collaborating from the data will allow you to be able to sense how the organisation is working or not working, and where to act on this knowledge to make an improvement. When considering an improvement, ask yourself the following.

1. What to Change?
2. What to Change to?
3. How to Change?

Then measure the results of the change to see if it worked or not. *If it hasn't worked, it's not a problem, just go again.*

TAKEAWAYS

- ⇨ Pain points can be gathered and visualised quickly.
- ⇨ Be curious about the cost and impact of waste.
- ⇨ Sense and visualise problems.
- ⇨ Waste can have different impact levels.
- ⇨ Some waste types are easier to remove than others.

CHAPTER 4
COMMERCIAL REASONS TO REMOVE WASTE

BY IMPLEMENTING THE METHODS AND VALUE streams, labs and teams capturing and removing waste, the word will start to spread across the organisation which is a good thing. As a CTO you want to increase the pace of meaningful products to customers as quickly to be as efficient and effective as possible. However the words, waste and delay may then generate some other questions from areas such as Business Management. These could come in the form of:

"So then how much money are we going to be able to save?"

At this stage, you may not be able or even want to answer those questions as the focus is on making the organisation as efficient and effective as possible.

The next chapter looks at some methods and techniques, where your agile coaches and scrum masters could capture information in the work they are delivering via agile methods, so to enable the organisation to capture flow rates and waste information a language that can be used between yourself and business management. This will show how flow, waste and finances can be discussed, bringing business management closer to the method you are trying to scale.

KEY CONCEPTS

The world has faced many challenges, but few greater than putting a person on the moon. Achieving this ambition involved solving thousands of individual problems, but all of these got solved because everyone involved was united by a common goal.

There is a great story to illustrate this. When US president John F. Kennedy toured NASA in 1962, seven years before Neil Armstrong stepped onto the lunar surface, he stopped to ask a janitor, "What do you do?" The reply, "I am helping put a man on the moon," clearly stated the main objective. But while the overall goal was abundantly clear, what was the commercial rationale for such a risky and expensive endeavour?

At the time, the commercial goal took second place to politics. The immediate advantages were perceived as:

- Boosting national pride for everyone by being first to the moon
- Beating the Soviet Union...

... and not necessarily in that order.

Longer term, arguably the main benefits turned out to be:

- Paving the way for space travel and an international space station.
- Developing satellite TV and communications technology such as international calling and global positioning (GPS) in mobile phones that all of us enjoy.

This brave objective opened up markets for other technologies developed for the programme, including breathing apparatus and protective clothes, solar panels, fire retardant equipment, and artificial limbs. Such spin-offs are used in industries all around the world and still benefit us 50 years later.

In hindsight, the commercial benefits were huge but they never would have happened if America's leaders had got cold feet. If Kennedy had declared that it would cost too much money or NASA had objected on the grounds that it had never tried anything remotely as ambitious, none of that potential would have been realised.

In reality, of course, the project was funded by the American people through their taxpayer dollars. So Kennedy had to make the case to them to justify this extravagant spend. To do this, he presented the moon landing as an opportunity to secure America's future. Senior leaders, too, should lean towards the positive and embrace the opportunities when discussing waste rather than presenting it as a problem to solve. When you have lemons, sell lemonade.

Some senior leaders find this hard. With every decision there are risks, rewards, costs and consequences. It's easy to see why a leader would fall back on what they've done before. That's why it's so difficult to convince a senior leadership team with traditional values and behaviours to adopt the idea of looking for, and removing, waste. All is not lost, however. In the next chapter, we will look at some tried and trusted techniques that will leave you better equipped for the conversations you'll have with senior leaders.

But first let's circle back to the moon landing. Although removing waste and the Apollo missions aren't superficially similar, you can get senior leaders to think about immediate benefits and longer-term benefits in much the same way.

Immediate benefits:

- Know where the interaction and pain points (waste) that exist between teams and labs.

- Measure of how many days are lost to waste.
- Measure of the amount of work blocked.

Longer term benefits:

- Ability to increase the pace of products to customers.
- Increase the delivery capacity.
- Improve team and lab morale by removing friction and pain points.

Figure 4.1. Finances, pace of delivery and cost is good information to know how the organisation is performing.
Image by aurielaki / Shutterstock.com

You can tell a lot about senior leaders' mindset from their language. When I hear members of a senior leadership team saying things like, "I have done this before" or "I'm an expert in this area", it can indicate vulnerability. Their immediate reaction is to challenge the numbers and the methods required to reduce waste, even after being presented with eye-opening data collected from their own company. However, trying something new needs an open-minded leader, whether it's finding and removing waste or landing on the moon.

Ideally, of course, senior leaders should be open. They should want to understand the data to see if there's an opportunity to improve their business. Your challenge as a CTO is to get their support to embed your ideas into the culture of the organisation.

There will be some that aren't open to change and new methods. They may not have the mindset to embrace change, so instead you should seek out open-minded senior leaders. But even if they are open-minded, you'll still need to convince them that it's the right thing to do by helping them understand the commercial benefits.

One way of doing this is to incorporate the flow rate of value products to customers and align it to the waste that impacts productivity. The organisation can view the flow rate of value to customers and waste knowledge together to see how it could impact finances of the organisation. This will start to show the impact on pace of delivery to customers, and the costs of the capacity lost. Later in the book will look at a Knowledge Repository and Information that could help.

TRADITIONAL WATERFALL

In a traditional waterfall world, it was much easier for Business Management to understand and account for funding. When something went into deployment, it could be capitalised and then depreciated over time. However, in adaptive, agile ways of working with regular delivery and experiments with prototyping, spikes as well as deployment of useful code to customers are all happening at the same time. This blurs the lines between the value delivery to customers that can be capitalised by Business Management who manage finance and operations costs such as training, design, spikes and prototypes.

Due to making it harder for Business Management to understand and account for, the agile ways of working are harder to understand from the cost perspective.

The main concern is, of course, delivering value in the most efficient way to our customers, to make the best use of the transformational budget. So being able to converse with Business Management about flow, value, waste, capitalisation and operation costs is helpful, especially if the organisation is starting to move from a traditional waterfall way of working to an adaptive, agile way of working.

WHAT CAN WE DO ABOUT IT USING AGILE METHODS?

One way of thinking about it is to consider an epic or user story as value, setting up a meeting with Business Management and looking at the types of work the teams deliver. Then work with Business Management to work out if they see these as operational costs (Opex) or items of value the customer can use. If so, they are therefore able to capitalise them (Capex), thus writing off the costs over a number of years,

Let's look at some example work items:

- User story that delivers value to the customer — Capitalisation cost — (Capex)
- User story that delivers a design — Operation cost — (Opex)
- Team Training week — Operation cost — (Opex)
- Spike - Task to Answer a question — Operation cost — (Opex)[11]

The items above are made up, but if you take these to Business Management, they can advise which work can be capitalised and which are operational costs.

---

[11] https://agiledictionary.com/209/spike/

The next stage is to write these into a checklist for the scrum masters, so each user story as it flows through to be delivered is marked as either Capex or Opex. By giving each user story a clear indication of value and a description of what makes it an operational or a capitalisation cost, it allows us to see the pace of value flowing through the organisation's system of change.

Revisit these items on the scrum masters' checklist with the Business Management and adjust accordingly, so that Business Management and scrum masters can see how it relates back to value.

Then by using a workflow engine such as Jira, the organisation can start to build up the following information:

- Flow rates of user stories.
- Delays (time lost) caused by waste.
- Percentage split of work delivered (Capex versus Opex)

- Cost per user story by Team / Lab / Value Stream.
- Cost per epic by Team / Lab Value Stream.

This allows you, as a CTOs, to start using the language of Business Management to explain the impact of blockages and waste in the system. This might feel a bit scary to them initially, as no one wants to know how ugly their baby is, in terms of how the organisation runs. But now that we have the information, it can act as an aid to show how we can continually improve how the organisation runs, thus reducing waste and increasing the amount of value delivered to customers.[12]

I am not an accountant, but being able to start having conversations with finance helps bring them onto the same page.

The ability to explain the time it takes to get value to the customers, and how it aligns to Capex and Opex, will facilitate conversations between Agile teams and Business Management. Showing how much

---

[12] https://en.m.wikipedia.org/wiki/Capital_expenditure
https://en.m.wikipedia.org/wiki/Operating_expense

waste is in the system of change also starts to paint a picture of the opportunity to improve the organisation by delivering more value to customers at no additional cost. This is very useful when trying to influence those higher up in the organisation.

Business Management can now start to answer some questions such as :

- What is the speed to Market for Customer Value?
- What is the percentage split of Capex Costs versus Opex Costs?
- What is the percentage of time spent on value versus time blocked via waste?
- How many days work is blocked due to waste in the organisation?
- What is your flow rate of products to customers versus costs?

Traditional leaders tend to struggle with Agile examples from change professionals. So, the message here is to try to put it into their language while also focusing on the waste and its impact on the flow of products to customers.

The outcome any senior leader is looking for is: how do I encourage my leadership team to have skin in the game? How do I make them, and the teams and labs in the work, accountable?

An area to be wary of is existing Service Level Agreements, which can act against delivering value to customers as quickly and efficiently as possible.

Service level agreements

Organisations generally have embedded service level agreements (SLAs) to show how well they are performing. For example, Team A must respond back to Team B within three days. Typically, they'll have a lot of green (good) status SLAs and leaders would, quite rightly, think they are great and their organisation is knocking it out of the park. But let's look at this in a little more detail.

Have you ever had to deal with an organisation and had a service level agreement quoted back to you? Something like, "It is our SLA to have that back to you within 3 days." This allows the organisation to take up to 3 days to complete the task for you. However, this doesn't allow the view of the end-to-end time of the works and how much time is spent delivering value and how much time is delivering waste.

Let's look at an example below, with an SLA of 3 days to complete a task for a customer:

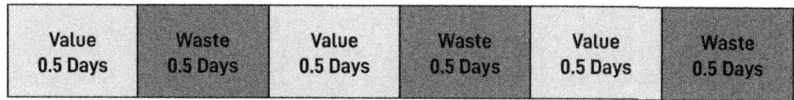

Figure 4.2. Value and Waste on a Service Level Agreement (SLA) timeline

The embedded service level agreements (SLAs) will show that delivering the piece of work to the customer is a 100% success as we did not exceed their 3 days to complete the piece of work.

Now, by using the flow rate and time spent on value and waste, let's look at the same example in the diagram above:

- 50% of the time is wasted due to blocked work.
- 50% of the time is spent delivering value.

Now with your finance hat on, are you OK with reporting SLA's when you know that 50% of your capacity is being sapped due to work being blocked.

Now this actually gets worse as it creates other behaviours when work gets blocked. Team members can pick up other work, which increases work in progress, which also slows the pace of delivery.

The above is a general fictional representation of how work can stop and start, where using The Waste Detectives Methods as a measurement of value capacity and waste capacity can be obtained. The more value capacity we can use in the transformation journey the better, as this allows more value to be released to customers.

Now let's look at some scenarios to illustrate Service Level Agreements (SLA).

Team Alpha consists of developers who, on occasion, need access to a database administrator (DBA) in Team Bravo. The developer in Team Alpha has produced the code and just needs a DBA to perform a database job that takes five minutes to run.

Scenario 1

Service Level Agreement (SLA) to complete the works: 600 minutes

The developer asks the DBA to perform a task. The DBA explains that they are busy on another task and will add the work to the product backlog. As the Service Level Agreement (SLA) approaches, they pick up the work and complete the task. The work is completed within the Service Level Agreement (SLA) and both tasks are completed for the customer. The developer's time to make the change is 10 minutes, but they have had to wait 4 hours (240) minutes for the DBA. The code is finally live in a total time of 300 minutes.

Behaviours:

- The Developer in Team Alpha stops working on something due to a blockage, generating waste in the system of change. The work-in-progress increases and the developer starts to multi-task. This, in turn, slows the delivery rate of the product to the customers.
- Leaders are happy as all the reporting metrics of the SLA are green. The system is performing well!
- Customers are unhappy as they have had to wait three days for the development to be completed so they can use the product.

This is one piece of code. Imagine if you had 10,000 or even 40,000 developers. How slow is the work and how much capacity is being lost?

Scenario 2

Service Level Agreement (SLA) to complete the works: 600 minutes

The developer asks the DBA to perform a task. The developer is available and completes the task in 10 minutes and the code is live 60 minutes later.

Behaviours:

- The developer in Team Alpha completes the work and collaborates when needed. They are happy the job is done and value is released.
- Leaders are happy as all the reporting metrics of the Service Level Agreements (SLA) are green. The system is performing even better!
- Customers are impressed that the code is released so quickly.

Commercially, even if the Service Level Agreements (SLAs) are all green, the organisation is potentially still not performing well. Knowing the time it takes to deliver value to your customers and the percentage of waste versus value work is more important.

Knowing how teams multitask on several items of work at the same time and hand off work to each other affects the bottom line in terms of dollars or pounds. How can you help senior leaders maximise the investment being put into building and maintaining products for customers?

When you hear everything is fine and that they are within Service Level Agreements (SLAs), it should make your ears prick up. These are potentially good areas to start looking for waste and delays to the flow of value products to customers.

Service Level Agreements (SLA) do not show you how well the organisation is performing.

As a CTO, start by looking at flow rate of value to customers and the wasted time and capacity sapping the flow and pace of delivery across the organisation as a whole from value stream, lab and teams.

This could help you prove the efficiency level of how well you are performing as a lab or team in delivering value to customers.

Plus by knowing the operation (Opex) and capitalisation (Capex) costs, it will provide you with more of an insight into how the organisation is performing and where, as a leader, to focus your time to make improvements to the organisation.

If you are in an organisation where all the SLAs are green, follow a piece of work from start to finish and see how long it takes to get from the ideas phase into the customer's hands. How much of the time was working time and how much of the time was waiting (waste) time?

Look out for the touch points of the work between teams, waiting times and blockers (waste).

WHY IS THIS IMPORTANT?

The organisation you're advising could be wasting at least 50% of its capacity. It could even be as high as 70%. This could be sapping a lot of capacity and incurring unnecessary extra costs and expenditure.

The amount of potential waste and capacity being sapped determines how many products you can deliver versus your transformational budget.

The service level agreements currently being used are all tracking positive management information to senior leaders. However, the blockages and waste in the organisation design prevents valuable products being delivered to customers in a timely manner. This may not be something that is currently recognised as people get used to delays in systems. How often have we queued up at the post office and just accepted the delay as normal? It is potentially what your organisation and those within it accept as OK. Later we will look at how building a knowledge repository can reveal where to make improvements in order to remove waste and improve capacity.

HOW A CTO CAN USE THESE TECHNIQUES

The CTO can explain to value streams, labs and teams why being able to capture information in a language that the business management (finance) functions can understand. Allow the waste detective's language to align with that of business management.

This will also show how moving from being a traditional thinking to an adaptive (digital) organisation may (if it hasn't already) include how we use information such as flow, waste, capex and opex together.

SUMMARY

The ability to show flow, waste and financial information together allows a measurement approach to be in place to see how efficient and effective the organisation is at delivering value to customers. Later in the book a knowledge repository will be covered to show how this information can be obtained and used within the organisation.

TAKEAWAYS

⇨ Leverage commercial reasons to want to find and remove waste.
⇨ Leverage commercial reasons to continually improve.
⇨ Make senior leaders through to team members accountable for removing waste and continually improving.
⇨ Trust Service Level Agreements (SLAs) at your peril.
⇨ Green SLAs will not show the location of pain and capacity being lost in the organisation.
⇨ Ask yourself what Service Level Agreements (SLA) give you!

CHAPTER 5
KNOWLEDGE REPOSITORY & INFORMATION

SO FAR, THE BOOK HAS COVERED the need to influence, leaders needing to act on knowledge (data), the waste detective methods and how to add an additional technique to capture information for those who look after the finances in the transformation you are leading as a CTO.

Teams are now up and running collecting and acting on waste knowledge (data) and removing locally within teams and labs. Now to leverage this at scale, let's consider the concept of building a waste knowledge repository that collects this information. Allowing you as a CTO working with your peers at director level, plus the value stream leads who are becoming adaptive leaders and wanting to act on the waste knowledge (data) to improve the performance of the organisation.

KEY CONCEPTS

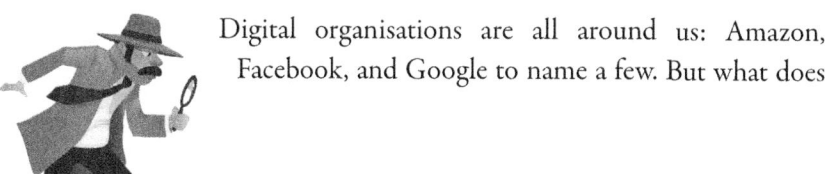

Digital organisations are all around us: Amazon, Facebook, and Google to name a few. But what does that mean? A good way of thinking about it is explained in the following data driven quote. [13]

> *"Being a data-driven organisation means culturally treating data as a strategic asset and then building capabilities to put the asset to use, not just for big decisions but also for everyday action on the front line."*

I am sure we have all logged into our smartphones and an advert pops up with something we like. That is no surprise. The data is being used in the background and leveraged to boost sales.

I imagine that even Tony is getting some updates on his mobile phone about special offers on jeans now and then!

Having access to waste data to make decisions can improve capacity if you are fortunate enough to be using an agile tool with a database capability. You then have the means to capture the data you require in the work via your feature teams and labs.

Waste knowledge can be captured manually via the techniques previously covered. However, the power of data across the organisation for making decisions is where you'll want to get to as a leader. So let's have a look at some areas to consider in this journey.

DATA SOURCES

Information (data) is gold dust, but in order to get access to the gold, you'll need sound data. The Waste Detective Methods provides guidance on how teams and labs can capture this information whilst in the

---

[13]   https://en.wikipedia.org/wiki/Data-driven

work as part of their daily activities. We will cover how you can measure how mature your teams are at capturing data and acting on the data in the work. But let's consider some of the data you may require. Your organisation may require more; this is just a guide to help get you started.

The information in agile tools, such as Jira is recorded in a database, a storage area of information capturing the work flowing using techniques to customers. A database can be a good source of information for a knowledge repository.

In order to get some meaningful and useful waste data from your agile waste knowledge repository, the following source data items could be considered for work that is blocked, either in an agile tool or manually.:

- Unique Identifier
- Team name
- Description of the work
- Date and time work stopped (due to blocker)
- Date and time work started (after blocker removed)
- Time lost due to waste
- Description of why work was blocked (who, what, impact)
- Description of how waste was resolved and removed.
- Theme or cluster of waste type grouping

Unique Identifier

Being able to uniquely identify a piece of work can be done automatically by agile tools. But if one isn't available, consider the ability to create a unique id. This will help identify and pinpoint work that is blocked and ensure that teams and leaders are all talking about the same work. This will also help with grouping and aggregating the data in reports at a later stage.

Team Name

This allows the consumer of the information to see which team has been blocked. It's very useful because you can group the data by team and the team has the ability to group and consume their own data, which is useful because experienced teams can have different problems that are blocking and sapping their capacity. Aggregating at a higher level might not show you where the problems are. Capturing at team level will allow you to operate at a team level and lab or value stream level at a later stage via the reporting.

Description of the work

This is a description of the value work that is being currently blocked. This could be a user story using typical style such as this one from scrum. org: As a <stakeholder> I want <a feature> so that <Need / Problem to solve>. [14]

It could include acceptance criteria of what "done" looks like, maybe using the gherkin or cucumber approach. [15]

Understanding the description of the work will allow you to know what type of work is blocked, what other work it is potentially linked to, and what value is prevented from being delivered to the customer.

Date and Time work stopped (due to blocker)

Knowing the date and time the work could not be worked on allows you to start building this into measures to help understand the consequences

---

[14] https://www.scrum.org/resources/blog/user-story-or-stakeholder-story
[15] https://www.scrum.org/resources/blog/simple-example-definition-done#:~:text=Acceptance%20criteria%20are%20an%20optional,%2C%20customer%2C%20or%20other%20stakeholder.

of the problem, such as being able to count how many items of work are blocked and the number of days work has not been able to progress.

Date and Time work started (after blocker removed)

Knowing the date and time the work could not be worked on allows you to start building this into some measures to help understand the consequences of the problem. This data is used to capture the end date for how long the work was stopped.

Time Lost due to Waste (Days, Hours, Seconds)

A measure of how long work has been stopped using a formula like this:

(Time between Date and Time work stopped (due to blocker) and Date and Time work started (after blocker removed)
or
(Time between Date and Time work stopped (due to blocker) and Today's Date

Description of Why work is blocked

A detailed description of the reason why work cannot be progressed can help teams and leaders understand where the bottlenecks are.
　　Use the Who / What / Impact from Waste Detectives Methods.

Example:

WHO: The Value Stream Team ABC

WHAT: The Team ABC does not have the developer to complete code that allows the feature to be delivered allowing customers to pay using their smart watches.

IMPACT: xxx number of customers currently paying on a smart watch won't be able to pay for products on xxx date. This will have a serious impact on the company's brand image. We may lose customers.

CATEGORY (Cluster): Within a resource team.

Description of how blockage was resolved

A detailed description of how waste (blocker) was removed. This provides knowledge of how problems are currently being resolved and may highlight an area for improvement.

Category of Waste Type grouping

- Within the team
- External to team (within same company)
- Third Party Company
- Technical
- Governance
- Data
- Other

Note: Personally, I try to limit the number of themes or clusters to 7 +/- 2 for usability reasons. If you have too many (more than 9), it becomes unusable. Remember that themes or clusters just help you know where to fish for waste.

SOLUTION EXPLORATION & EXPERIMENTATION

Start small with groups of aligned individuals and teams who want to work and solve the problems and achieve the vision as we explored in chapter 2. Set up a series of experiments along the way and potentially try a number of options. Then gather feedback from those in the work, creating solutions for the users to help find and remove waste as well as the customers of the work such as scrum masters, product owners and agile coaches and many more.

Experiments allow you to learn and adapt as you go. This will allow many ideas, views and learning to be brought together to fairly quickly improve the waste knowledge repository solution. Then as you go, validate whether the experiments have been a success or not.

As you experiment, think of the following: what is the current state now, what do you want to learn, what are the next steps, and what is expected? Finally, at the end of the experiment, look at what you have learnt. Later in the chapter we will have a look at an experiment template in more detail.

Example:

- The current state is that we are only able to find the number of days of waste for a whole area.
- We want to be able to deliver the number of waste days lost per team.
- The next step is to create a solution where the waste days can be aggregated per team.
- We expect the teams to want and use this information locally to work on removing waste at a team level.
- We learnt that a particular field in the data source needs to be used for teams and this would need comms and training in order to scale the solution wider.

DATA QUALITY

In Chapter 6, we will talk about the maturity level of the team, lab and value stream required to capture and act on The Waste Detectives Methods knowledge. When you start capturing that knowledge as an organisation, some of it may not be at the quality level you'll need to get the knowledge from the data.

This process is a journey for the whole of the organisation. Over time it's important to bring people with you and explain why the information is important. Be curious and allow the scrum masters to build capability and be aware that the waste data knowledge is useful for all levels: team, lab and value stream.

There are measures you can add based on the data to help understand where you are, data quality-wise, such as Theme (Cluster) quality in the figure below. From the dataset, you could apply business rules to look for when no Theme (Cluster) information has been added.

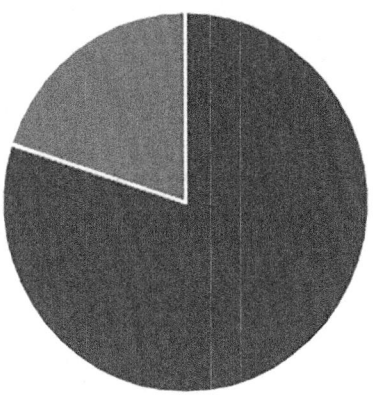

Figure 5.1 : Waste theme cluster quality

Another area similar to the one above is adding a rule to see if no knowledge information has been captured. You'll be able to adjust your dataset rule according to how you set up the capturing of your waste knowledge.

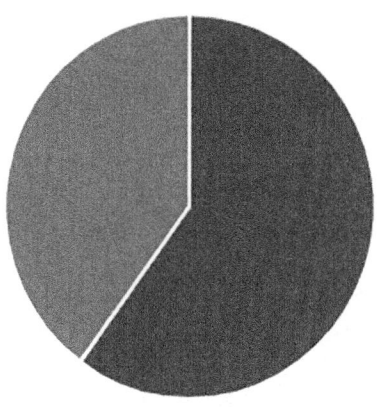

Figure 5.2 : Waste Knowledge Data Quality

WASTE KNOWLEDGE FROM DATA REPOSITORY

The ability of having a waste knowledge data repository is that all your fish are contained in the same area and accessible to catch. The waste knowledge data repository can, at a high level, start to split the waste into size buckets using the theme (cluster) information that we discussed above in the source data section. Let's look at some examples below.

Theme of Waste by Team

The source data can give you the number of days that work is blocked, the team name and the Theme (Cluster). By accessing this data, you can start to see pockets of information. It won't show you what's wrong, but it will show you how to see where the potentially bigger problems are, to look deeper at the detailed information.

Bar Chart by Team

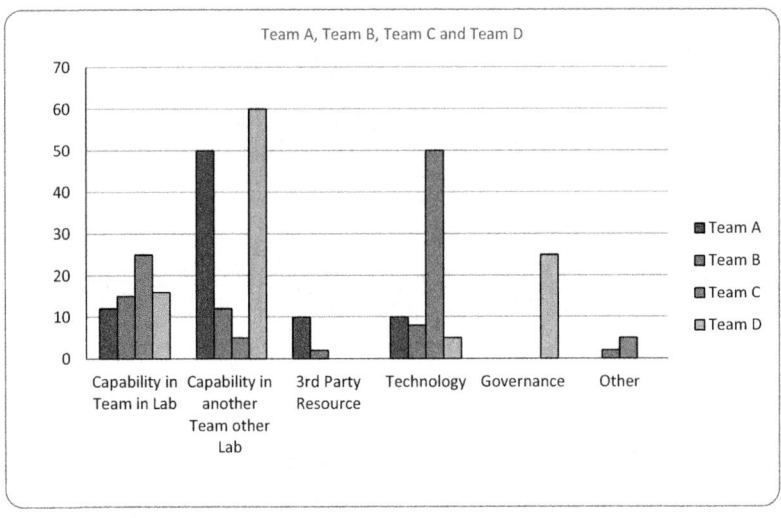

Figure 5.3 : Number of Days Blocked by Team by Waste Theme

From the chart above as a digital leader, where would you focus first and why?

We can also produce trend analysis in relation to the number of blocked items or blocked days per sprint at a team, lab or value stream level. Figure 5.4, shows an example of blocked items per sprint. Other chart types are available, this is just for illustration purposes.

Trending charts or plotting to see if waste is getting better or worse can be useful to see trends, but having only numbers doesn't give you knowledge of why. You would hope that as you experiment and continuously improve the organisation to reduce waste, the trend would reduce. But as you are scaling teams into capturing more and more information, these numbers might trend upwards to start with.

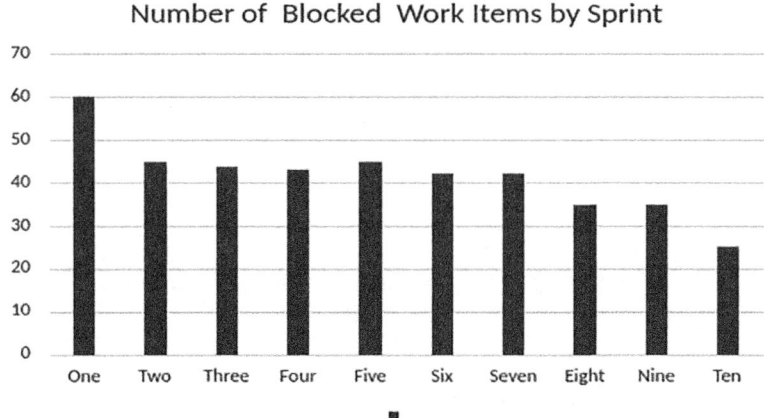

Figure 5.4 : Number of Blocked Work Items by Sprint

Pie Chart by Theme

Pie charts are also great visual tools. Here we have an example using the source data above, showing the number of blocked days for a team. It shows us that the highest number of days delay and sapping capacity is down to capability outside of the team or lab. This allows us to want to sense the data we look at. This lower-level knowledge will allow you to see how much those pain points are hurting the flow of meaningful products to customers.

This demonstrates where you might want to start looking for more information in order that you can act on your system of change team, lab or value stream in order to make performance improvements.

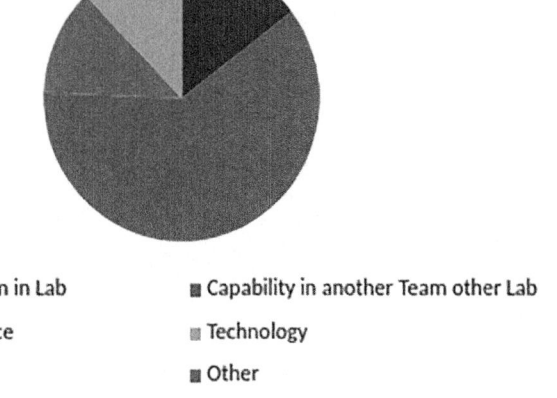

Number of Days Blocked by Teams by Waste Theme

- Capability in Team in Lab
- 3rd Party Resource
- Governance
- Capability in another Team other Lab
- Technology
- Other

Figure 5.5 : Number of Days Blocked by Teams by Waste theme

WORD CLOUD OF WASTE KNOWLEDGE

Word cloud technology is available in some management information tools by capturing the "Description of why work is blocked" in the source data. You'll be able to pull out the main words aligned to either the number of days blocked or the number of work items blocked. The bigger the word, the bigger the number in the data. It's a great way to keep those aware of what the most common form of waste is in the team, lab or value stream who need and act on the information.

By looking at the illustration below, we can quite quickly see that the highest number of tickets or number of days lost due to work not moving (depending on how it is configured) shows that "Development" is the largest form of waste. This is a made-up example but it illustrates how the knowledge you are capturing can be turned into useful management information.

It's a good idea to build a waste knowledge repository for the whole organisation at first. Then you could set up filtering by team and/or division. This is a really powerful way to help digital minded leaders who are looking to continually improve the organisation.

Note: business rules can be used to exclude words over time that add no value.

Figure 5.6 : Waste Word Cloud
Image by Image by Boris15 / Shutterstock.com

QUESTIONS A KNOWLEDGE REPOSITORY CAN HELP YOU ANSWER

As a CTO running the workshop or session with a value stream, you may want to address questions like the ones below:

Where is the largest Theme of waste in my team / lab?
    Bar / pie charts and word clouds can visually show that.
What Theme of waste is worst per team / lab
    Bar / pie charts and word clouds can visually show that.

Then when the waste data is surfaced, assist them in creating experiments to try and remove the waste. Measuring the results of the experiment.

FINANCE MEASURES FROM DATA REPOSITORY

Build a bar or pie chart to show the percentage of work delivered that was aligned to operation (costs) versus those that aligned to capitalisation costs (Capex). It can also show a breakdown of work that was delivered with a split of value and waste time associated.

DECISION MAKING

Using the knowledge repository and being able to access the data to ask the questions about what is slowing the pace of delivery puts you in a great place to make an intervention and a change.
Following the steps.

- What do I want to change?
- What do I want to change to?
- How am I going to change?

The waste knowledge repository will allow you and the teams and labs to see if that change has worked or not.

EXPERIMENTS

Once you have decided what to change and how you want to change it, write that up as a core belief (hypothesis) or experiment (the phrase

I personally prefer). This can be done in many formats, but let's look at one type of experiment template.

Problem	Experiment	Verification - we will	Measure	Right if the following
Why the waste blockers in the system are a problem.	A core belief that if we make a change via this hypothesis / experiment then the following will be true.	The way in which we are going to verify if the experiment has worked or not worked.	How you are going to measure the results of the experiment.	If the following points are true then we would have confirmed the experiment has been a success.

Table 5.1 : Experiment Template

And now here's an example of this in action.

Problem	Experiment	Verification - we will	Measure	Right if the following
Team ABC in value stream Z has repeatedly been blocked by third party AAA due to the third party not having sufficient database administration resources available. The team is trying to deliver product A, resulting in 150 days of waste and delay to flow.	We believe that having database administration resources available will allow a smooth flow of products to customers and the amount of waste in the system for Team ABC will be reduced in relation to third party database administration resources.	The Team ABC will measure the flow rates of the work through to customers, using a scatter chart if using Kanban or a control chart if using scrum. The team will look for any outliers, using the waste knowledge repository to look for waste in relation to third-party database administration resources. The team will set a marker when the experiment commences.	Team ABC will measure the flow rates of products to customers for x weeks and look back and compare it to flow data before the change. The team will measure the waste data available in the waste data knowledge repository as detailed above.	The flow of work items that needed to have database administration resources has improved. The amount of waste has been reduced.

Table 5.2 : Experiment Template

CONTINUOUS IMPROVEMENT

Once you have completed the experiment, go back to the waste knowledge and decide what you are going to change next. We are looking to continually improve working towards our vision of finding and removing waste.

To improve, we need to **plan** what we want to change following Process Improvement Methodology (Figure 5.7). In this chapter, we have looked at using the knowledge repository to come to the decision of what to change, what to change to, and how to change it. Once we knew what we wanted to change, we wrote that up into a hypothesis or experiment. We did the experiment (**do**) and then did a results **check** of the experiment to see if it had worked or not. We can then try a new experiment if this one fails, or go back to the waste knowledge repository and decide what we want to do next in terms of deciding what to change. [16]

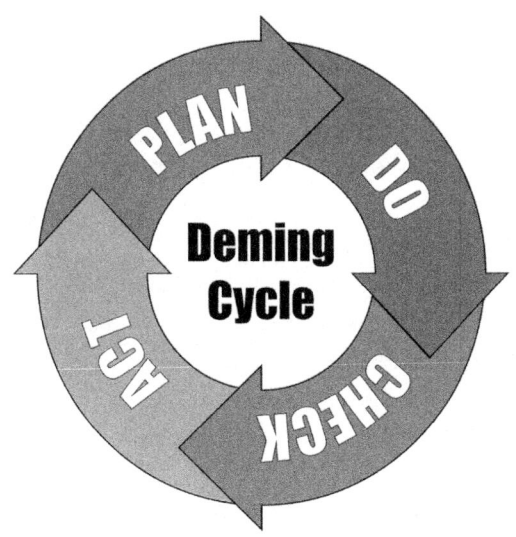

Figure 5.7 : Plan, Do, Check, Act (PCDA)
Process Improvement Methodology
Image by Jaiz Anuar / Shutterstock.com

---

[16] https://deming.org/explore/pdsa/

BEHAVIOURS

Teams and labs will welcome leaders in the work working with them to solve problems and produce experiments. The behaviours we are seeking are curiosity and wanting to continually improve via experimentation.

Traits of leaders with poor behaviours are command and control and micromanaging. This might provide insight into individuals who are not the right people to be digital minded leaders for you in the future.

EXERCISE

Part 1

1. Have a value stream and labs who are using an agile method such as kanban or scrum start to capture what is blocking the work. They will capture the waste data source, which they could do manually to start with:
   a. Capture
      i. Unique Identifier
      ii. Team name
      iii. Description of the work
      iv. Date and Time work stopped (due to blocker)
      v. Date and Time work started (after blocker removed)
      vi. Time lost due to waste
      vii. Description of why work is blocked
      viii. Description of how blockage was resolved
      ix. Theme or Cluster of waste type grouping
2. Hold a workshop with the information captured. Bring in the business lead, decision makers and the whole of the team, including the agile coaches who are embedding The Waste Detectives Methods.
3. Put all of the waste data up on the walls, printed on separate cards.

4. Build a bar chart of Themes off the raw data and show it to all.
5. Build a bar chart / pie chart of the number of days lost by sprint and by Theme (Cluster) and show it to all.
6. Build a word cloud of the common words of "why" and number of days lost for each reason.
7. Explain that we can carry on as we are and lose this capacity of work not flowing or we could make a change.
8. Ask all those in the room a question:
   a. We can carry on as we are or make a change. Vote now?

Outcome: All those in the work and the decision makers can see what's slowing the team down. Plus, you can see that everyone wants to make a change to make the working environment better.

PART 2

1. Print off the output bar and pie chart and word cloud on the wall of the workshop.
2. Give all those in the room 30 minutes to have a look at the information.
3. Have a suggestion box in the corner of the room ready.
4. Ask everyone in the room to write down what they would change, and why, on a card and put the idea in a box.
5. Put all ideas on the wall and give everyone three votes only to put on the one they'd like to change. They can allocate the three votes in any way they want to).
6. The three votes can be used all on one item, or split across more than 1 item.
7. Order the 'what to change' ideas in priority order of votes.
8. Ask the senior leader to make a decision of what they would like to change to improve the team/lab/value stream.
9. Write this up in the form of an experiment with your agile coaches.

Outcomes:

- Awareness of what is slowing the value stream and labs down.
- Early designs are generated quickly and collaboratively, see how they can visually land the message. These can later be designed into the knowledge repository.
- Leaders work with the team, making decisions to help improve the performance.
- There may be more data required than that of the source data alone. Add to the 'data you need' list.

PART 3

As CTO, hold a storytelling session with your peers who are potentially at director level from the waste knowledge captured in this exercise, expose the scale of the waste and the problems to the senior leaders in the organisation. You may get asked questions, so if we remove this waste how much can we save? The question you'd like them to ask is how much capacity can we get back and how much quicker can we deliver products to our customers?

Now use the measures of flow and the capitalisation of products delivered to customers. So, via The Waste Detectives Methods, you have a scaled method to answer and provide measurable knowledge on those points.

THE BIGGER ORGANISATIONAL PICTURE

The organisation will have a strategy that it is aiming to deliver, which could, for example, be to stay relevant to its current customer base. Then it would think about the next layer of products it needs to start producing as value-based products to customers. It would also look way into the future at what customers might want. This is where the likes of Nokia, Blockbuster and Kodak failed because they failed to keep an eye on the future and the competition.

A useful way of moving forward is to consider your existing customers and the problems you might face in achieving your strategy. You can break down your investment in different areas. For example, investment might be split as follows:

- Keeping the lights on, i.e. maintain what we have (60%)
- Build and represent new current products (25%)
- The future (15%)

The last thing the organisation wants is to become uncompetitive and irrelevant, so when using a view of data, digital minded leaders can sense and know where to act.

One example of this is Skype, which was a leader in the digital video industry. But once WhatsApp started a mechanism to send digital messages, the term "I'll Skype you" quickly disappeared. Now you'll hear people talk about setting up a let's set up a WhatsApp group and having a "WhatsApp call". We can only wonder why this happened, but this will continue to happen to organisations that do not have a firm grasp on what the organisation wants in the future. Sometimes, as customers, we don't even know what we want in the future. However, we as customers do know what we like when we see it, so find out through experiment.

Knowing what is blocked, the capacity lost, and how it affects the flow of work, is aligned to the organisation's strategy. Modelling the organisation data in a way to get answers to those tough questions is something to consider in the wider use of the waste knowledge repository.

HOW A CTO CAN USE THESE TECHNIQUES

By having a knowledge repository of waste across the whole organisation, the CTO benefits from an overarching view of the types of problems and interactions and pain points across a collection of value streams, labs and teams. Common themes of problems can start to emerge, where a problem is felt across a number of areas. This provides the opportunity to try and fix the problems at a higher level, where a problem to be fixed at a top level it is resolved acoss many at a lower level.

This still allows labs and teams to continually improve locally to find and remove waste to increase the pace of products to customers.

PRACTICAL STORY

Working with a senior leader in an organisation, by building a knowledge repository of waste data, it provided a visual representation of the amount of capacity being drained, preventing flow of products to customers. The traditional management approach of keeping colleagues busy, usually means that not value / prioritised work gets started, clogging up the system and delaying valuable items of work even further

Having already worked with this senior leader on adaptive leadership, they were well on the way to becoming a leader who acted on knowledge rather than their past experience or gut feel.

The senior leader had a hunger for knowledge and worked with their lab product owners to understand the data and work as an area to see what they could try in the form of an experiment, to remove some of the waste.

From a study of the waste data, one team in the lab was able to spot a change to implement to the structure of the team which they thought would benefit the flow of products to customers, they implemented this change, increased the flow of products to customers and removed waste and delay from this team by 20% over x weeks.

SUMMARY

The waste knowledge repository built for an organisation can be used with the flow data to be able to make visible how many days of work are being delayed, by theme of the issue, as well as the ability to see from the text captured via agile software such as Jira.

The visual representation of the problem will allow you as a CTO to make a decision based on data in terms of where you would like to focus resources such as agile coaches, system thinkers and scrum masters to see where we can make improvements to the organisation via experiments.

TAKEAWAYS

- ⇨ Data is gold dust and can help you drive performance through to increased capability.
- ⇨ A solid set of source data, enables key questions to be answered from the data.
- ⇨ Data quality can take time to establish. Use the waste maturity model to help.
- ⇨ Be in the work with your teams and labs.
- ⇨ Be curious and have a collaboration mindset.
- ⇨ Charts and word clouds are a great visual representation of the waste knowledge (data).
- ⇨ Act on the data and make changes for improvements with the teams/labs.
- ⇨ Hold sessions with some early data to create concepts for your waste knowledge repository designs.

CHAPTER 6
MATURITY MODELLING

So you as a CTO have started to influence the organisation and the senior leaders on a journey to becoming adaptive leaders and using a knowledge repository of waste data to find and remove friction and pain points to increase the flow of products to customers and increase the delivery efficiency.

However in order for The Waste Detectives Methods to scale across and down into the organisation, those persons in the organisation's value streams, labs and teams need the capabilities defined in The Waste Detectives Methods.

To scale you'll need the whole organisation eventually to have and use The Waste Detectives Methods, so how can you embed and track the level of capability maturity of The Waste Detectives Methods throughout the organisation. This chapter will cover that maturity modelling of The Waste Detectives Methods that increases the capability of the organisation in the use of The Waste Detectives Methods.

KEY CONCEPTS

To remove waste at scale and truly reap the benefits, organisations have to have maturity, with waste-finding methods embedded in them culturally from top to bottom.

Maturity is, of course, found at a personal level as well as an organisational one. An example of this is cricketer Ben Stokes, whose night out with a fellow player in 2017 ended up with punches being thrown. It catapulted Stokes into a media storm and subsequent court case, and his cricketing career was in the balance. Fast forward two years and Stokes scored the winning runs for England in cricket's World Cup. Later, Stokes was made England's test captain and in 2022, as a fully mature, determined individual, he hit the winning runs in another final - this time the Twenty20 World Cup.

Now I am not saying we need a punch up to find ourselves, but many of us have done things that we dwell on and learn from to become more mature. For an organisation to mature, we need to increase the capability. We need a willingness to let go of the past and look to the future, as Ben Stokes did. Increasing the level of maturity can make the organisation better by allowing it to continually improve and provide more capacity to deliver for customers.

The term 'maturity modelling' was coined in 1986 after funding from the U.S. Department of Defence, and related to the degree of optimisation of processes. For further reading consider reading Implementing the Capability Maturity Model, James R. Persse 2001. Later, in 2006, capability maturity model integration was developed by the Software Engineering Institute.

Its intended purpose was to improve the software engineering processes.[17]

In adaptive (agile) digital transformations, we can consider two indicators of how we are performing as an organisation, the first being a

---

[17] https://en.wikipedia.org/wiki/Capability_Maturity_Model

leading measure and the latter a lagging measure. The leading measure will look at how mature the organisation is at adopting particular methods and techniques such as those we covered. The latter could be measures such as the time it takes to get a product from the concept phase into the customer's hands.

As leading measures grow, it's a sign that the organisation is getting more mature.

The lagging measure should grow as the organisation gets more mature. If it correlates, it should result in the flow of products to customers increases.

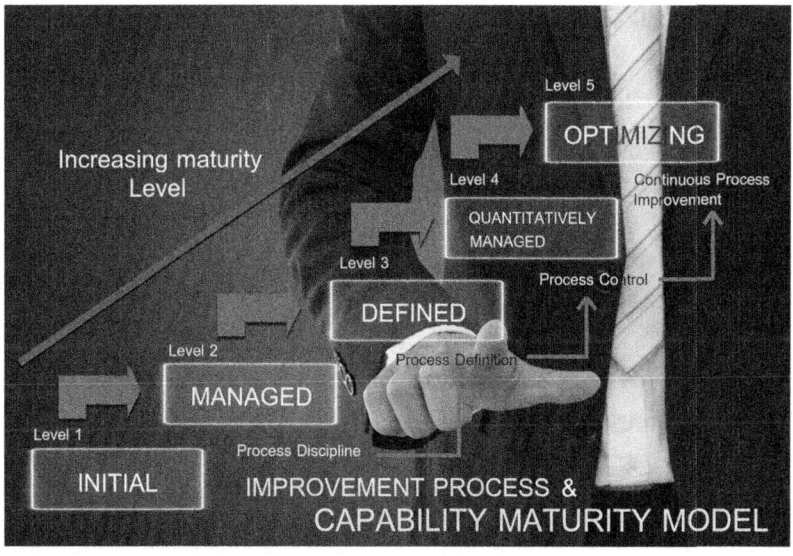

Figure 6.1 : Capability Maturity Model
Image by Keepsmiling4u / Shutterstock.com

Figure 6.1 above shows the series of stages for the improvement process and capability maturity model, through levels 1 to 5. It starts with the initial view, then progresses into managed, defined processes, quantitatively and then optimising for continuous improvement. In the next section, we will look at how you could build these stages to embed a maturity model for embedding the Waste Detectives methods and techniques into your organisation. You may be thinking why is this relevant to finding and removing waste, well in order to be able to find and remove waste, the organisation in which you are working needs to have a capability maturity in order to find and remove waste throughout it. We will cover this later in this chapter.

This all sounds great, but how can you achieve this to make it commercially viable to find and remove waste. What is the organisation going to have to put in place?

HOW TO ACHIEVE MATURITY

The goal is to help increase the organisation's level of maturity for finding and removing waste.

How are we going to achieve our end goal? Well, this is where you can leverage the scrum master community. scrum masters are in the organisation to lead and embed methods within the teams and organisation. As a CTO setting the strategy on finding and removing waste, you have the knowledge you want to spread across the whole organisation to a point where the maturity levels allow the organisation to deliver and continually improve.

scrum masters can help embed the capability model and build this in as a method in their tool kits. They can do this via training, podcasts, assigning them as champions in the methods of finding and removing waste, and using leading teams as living examples to showcase the expected behaviours. Then this capability can be grown across and throughout the organisation to embed continuous improvements.

Now, build a Waste Detectives capability model aligned to the organisation's leading and lagging performance measures. Forming a series of rungs on a ladder to achieve maturity, each of these rungs would hold the following. See below for an example.

These can be created in a sequence of cards that the feature team, labs and scrum masters can use to layer in, one at a time, in order to incrementally increase the capability of the teams and labs over a period of time. This can be measured by the organisation to get a measure of maturity for the Waste Detective methods. Remember to keep each level to an expected and tangible behaviour of minimise disputes in interpretation and prevent temptation to inflate "scores" over time.

HIGH-LEVEL EXAMPLES - WASTE DETECTIVES MATURITY CARD STEP

Details of example: The Waste Detectives Methods

Step Number : 1 of 5
Step Description : Recording waste data.
By using this technique from : Work recorded as blocked, is
the Waste Detectives visible to team members.
We will achieve this by the following : Number of days blocked per piece of work
We will know if we have achieved this by is known and number of items blocked.
Behaviour you would expect to see. : Teams are able to share what
work is being blocked.
: Teams are curious about what
is slowing them down.

Step Number : 1 of 5
Step Description : Recording waste data.
By using this technique from : Work recorded as blocked, is
the Waste Detectives visible to team members.
We will achieve this by the following : Number of days blocked per piece of work
We will know if we have achieved this by is known and number of items blocked.
Behaviour you would expect to see. : Teams are able to share what
work is being blocked.
: Teams are curious about what
is slowing them down.

Step Number	: 2 of 5
Description	: Recording waste data with knowledge.
By using this technique from the Waste Detectives	: Record specific knowledge of what waste is blocking teams from delivering.
We will achieve this by the following	: Teams record Who / What / Impact and Theme. Teams monitor and use the information.
We will know if we have achieved this by	: Teams will know why work is blocked and see patterns of what work is blocked.
Behaviour you would expect to see.	: Frustration that work is blocked and issues not being resolved with leaders' support.

Step	: 3 of 5
Description	: Sensing waste data.
By using this technique from the Waste Detectives	: Able to produce a bar chart of worst to least waste. Top impacts and pain known
We will achieve this by the following	: Teams record Who / What / Impact and Theme. Teams monitor and use the information
We will know if we have achieved this by	: Teams understand what is slowing the pace of products to customers.
Behaviour you would expect to see.	: Feeling of empowerment to make the working environment better.

Step	: 4 of 5
Description	: Identifying top blockers.
By using this technique from the Waste Detectives	: Will know lost days aligned to the value of products.
We will achieve this by the following	: Teams recording the impact of work lost, when work is blocked.
We will know if we have achieved this by	: An output waste (blocked) days per value can be produced.
Behaviour you would expect to see. Details of example : Chapter 2 (Top Blockers Experiment)	: Ability to enable future decision-making on what to improve first.

Step	: 5 of 5
Description	: Leadership Influence.
By using this technique from the Waste Detectives	: Leaders can make decisions on how and where to make improvements.
We will achieve this by the following	: Creating a culture of experimentation to improve how the team or team-to-team operate.
We will know if we have achieved this by	: Measure the waste metrics being captured by the teams.
Behaviour you would expect to see.	: Positive action being taken by leaders and teams to remove waste.

Summary Overview Lab Level Example

The diagram below shows how you could visualise the maturity level of The Waste Detectives Methods.

Lab Name: ABC Lab

Team 1 Maturity Level 1	Team 2 Maturity Level 2	Team 3 Maturity Level 4
Team 4 Maturity Level 3	Team 5 Maturity Level 5	Team 6 Maturity Level 2

Fig.6.2 Waste Maturity Model - Capability Matrix

Each colour can tie back to a colour code versus your maturity level. It acts as a really good visualisation of the maturity of each area of your business. (For those reading a paperback version - the Maturity Level Number)

LAGGING MEASURE

Were your organisation using a kanban system, you'd be limiting the work based on a pull-based system. Then having the blockers (waste) identified and blocker clustering as detailed in Essential kanban Condensed, David J Anderson and Andy Carmichael (2016)[18] [19]

You know, via the capability maturity, that you have the skills in your organisation and it is at maturity. But what is the real litmus test

---

[18] Essential Kanban Condensed, David J Anderson and Andy Carmichael (2016)
[19] The Waste Detectives Methods and Techniques Brian Hooker and Richard (Moir) (2021) Chapter 7

that your leadership and the continuous improvements have been successful at removing waste?

The Waste Detectives litmus test :

1. *Leadership Behaviour* change to enable capturing of waste knowledge (data).
2. *Team Behaviours* in collaboration to remove waste and experiment.
3. *Working as a unit* top to bottom and side to side.
4. *Waste Knowledge* Known
5. *Time to Customer* for meaningful product is measurable

LEADERSHIP BEHAVIOUR

Are the leadership curious and in the work with the team, not showing command and control behaviours? The leaders are working with the teams to understand the nature of the problems caused by the waste within it. The leaders are looking to experiment or perform interventions to act on the system of change and lab to make improvements. They are thinking about:

- What to change?
- What to change to?
- How to change?

The leaders are confident of attempting an improvement action to the lab or value stream area, knowing that there are three possible outcomes of making the intervention:

- The change improves capacity and reduces waste.
- There will be no impact to the lab or value stream area.
- The change will make it worse.

In life, we have core beliefs that a change will make something better, but we can measure to see if those changes have indeed made a difference.

Your leaders can try to make improvements without fear from the top and ideally this is culturally encouraged in the organisation.

Leaders see waste as important to focus on and make it strategically and culturally important to everyone in the organisation. Not a small task, but it is achievable. Planting the seeds with a few open-minded leaders and proving that the concept of finding and removing waste works will allow it to grow and flourish.

TEAM BEHAVIOUR

Curiosity of how the team/platform is operating would be a good start behaviourally, with an openness to understand why things currently work in a certain way. There is a willingness to collaborate internally within teams and labs as well as externally with other teams/labs and potentially third parties.

With openness and a mindset of wanting to try and improve the system of change team or lab, teams can experiment to make a change to how their team or lab functions.

Record details in an experiment template with details such as:

- Problem description
- Experiment
- Verifying the result by
- Measure the results by
- Experiment is right if ....

The final behaviour would be to make this habit-forming and part of a desire to improve how they operate day-to-day.

WORKING AS A UNIT

Finding and removing waste is a team sport. You need team members collecting the knowledge of what is preventing the system of change lab and/or team delivering. But these individuals will want to see the leaders in the work acting on waste to make the organisation better at a team level. It's essential that they want to help, not blame, and work as a unit to make things better. Digital minded leaders and teams work together.

WASTE KNOWLEDGE KNOWN

Capturing knowledge will provide you with a core base of data. But your organisation may need more, so this is something to design in and enable your decision making.

Ensure the waste knowledge repository is searchable, so waste information can be searched and found.

The basic waste data will provide: date work stopped, Date work started, knowledge of who, what, impact and theming. Build a waste repository interface into the data to drive searching and making decisions on where to do:

- Local team-based experiments
- Systematic organisation-level problem identification, enabling problem solvers to find and remove waste across a number of teams and labs

The knowledge will allow the leaders to decide what to change in the system of change to drive improvements.

TIME TO CUSTOMER

As an organisation, you understand how long things take to get products to the customer. Waste saps capacity. The organisation is comfortable with being able to discuss waste, the consequences to its bottom line and what capacity is being sapped. It seems like an opportunity to make it better.

EXERCISE

Team Level

Select a team and a scrum master who is curious and wants to have a go at increasing the capability and find waste within a feature team.

1. Spend time with the scrum master to explain the concept of the waste maturity model and the leading and lagging measures of finding and removing waste in a team, lab, and throughout an organisation on a transformation journey.
2. Build up a laminated set of waste capability levels (above are just five examples; you should be able to come up with five steps from your experience in the work.
3. Hold a workshop with the team and if you can bring in the product owner.
4. Stick each of the laminated cards on a wall or positioned on the floor.
5. Present for 10-20 minutes on the concept of the waste capability model.
6. Ask each team member to stand next to their capability level.
7. Ask each team member to explain why they think they are at that level.

8. Obtain a combined team score and set that as the waste capability maturity level. This can be a baseline to work with. (Consider using the lowest for a chain is only as strong as its weakest link)
9. Work with the team to call out the actions the team can take to increase the score. Record these as waste capability improvement activities.
10. Every month, repeat this activity. Hopefully the maturity level increases and waste stopping the team decreases.

Note: With waste reducing, use the lagging and leading measures to see if you have increased the flow of products to customers. If you have then this can be written up as a case study to help with show-and-tells to influence the concept across the whole organisation.

VALUE STREAM LEVEL

1. Have the value stream lead and CTO, who are working as equals, present the concept of why finding and removing waste is strategically important to the organisation.
1. Have each team set up in a designated area of the room. Have each scrum master go through the team level exercise above. (You'll need to prepare the scrum master before the session.)
2. Each team completes the team exercise and you then have a baseline per team, lab and value stream to work from.
3. Have value stream lead discuss the scores and information captured with each team's scrum master.
4. Group the actions to see if there are any common themes.
5. Ask the scrum masters what they need from you.

Note: Repeat this exercise every quarter.

The outcome of the session is that all members know that finding and removing waste is important to the value stream.

HOW A CTO CAN USE THESE TECHNIQUES

By knowing which parts of the organisation are maturing the capability in the waste detective methods, will show which value streams, labs and teams are maturing and which are not. Where you have areas that are maturing, these will provide useful case studies to share with peers.

The outcome you are looking for is to spread the curiosity of The Waste Detectives Methods through all areas of the organisation to grow the circle of influence to embed finding and removing of waste to continually improve.

PRACTICAL STORY

Working with a scrum master lead who was embedding the waste methods capability maturity model across a number of teams. They held a workshop with all of the team scrum masters, producing a set of laminate cards on each waste detective's maturity level and putting them on the wall. They briefly discussed the concepts of waste and then asked each of the scrum masters to go and stand by the maturity level laminate card for which their team was currently.

This visually showed where each team was and who were further along the journey than others. Then the team scrum master who was more mature, explained how it felt for the team and lessons learnt along the way. This started the process of collaborating to help each other and their teams become more mature in The Waste Detectives Methods.

This increased The Waste Detectives Methods capability throughout those teams.

SUMMARY

The organisation and teams will not become fully mature overnight, there needs to be a willingness and mindset of those across the organisation to want to embed The Waste Detectives Methods. By building a waste maturity model, a set of stages for how you increase capability can be produced, adding a little bit of value at each stage. To increase capability and also increase the awareness and influence the usage of The Waste Detectives Methods.

TAKEAWAYS

- ⇨ Capability maturity models are a leading indicator.
- ⇨ The capability maturity has a correlation to the lagging measures such as pace of delivery.
- ⇨ Scrum masters enable the capability to mature in your organisation.
- ⇨ Capability can be measured, so you can see how leaders and teams are performing.
- ⇨ Capability matures over time and this is a continual aspect of the organisation.
- ⇨ Need for openness to talk about the organisational problems waste causes.
- ⇨ Establish a baseline of waste capability at team, lab and value stream level.

CHAPTER 7
PAIN & INTERACTIONS

DELIVERING PRODUCTS TO CUSTOMERS AS EFFICIENTLY is what you'll want as CTO. The pain and interaction problems caused by waste and blockers, will make that slower and affect the capacity in how much your organisation can deliver.

In this chapter, the book will cover how an organisation's design may not be set up to achieve the goal of fast flow of products to customers. Looking into how the waste detectives methods can highlight where the pain and frictions points exist within your current organisational design. This allows you as a CTO with senior leaders to perform interventions to change the organisational design incrementally to improve the flow of products to customers.

On closer inspection, this means that adaptive leaders have 2 important jobs they must do:

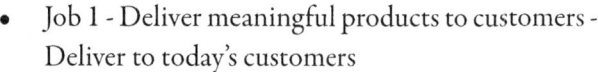

- Job 1 - Deliver meaningful products to customers - Deliver to today's customers
- Job 2 - Improve the system: Continuously improve - Ensure we are ready to deliver to tomorrow's customers.

KEY CONCEPTS

Delivering products to customers using agile methods often requires a team to get parts of their work done by other teams in the same organisation or via third party companies.

When work is handed off to other teams or organisations is problematic to flow and can be where pain points and interactions are created. The other teams may not have sufficient resource capacity to pick up and complete the work they are needed to perform. This will result in the work waiting, causing waste that prevents value flowing. It can cause delays and block the work in the team that needs the resource to be completed.

These pain points can be for a variety of reasons such as but not limited to:

1. The team or third party needing to do the work had no visibility of the request, so needed time to plan the work.
2. Capacity constraints on that resource type, needed to complete the work.
3. Different teams may have different local priorities, despite the best intentions at organisational alignment.

This results in the work blocked, causing pain in the interactions that slows the pace of delivery and saps capacity resulting in waste.

The Waste Detectives Methods allows you to find those pain points and interaction friction points between teams within and outside of the organisation. It allows leaders to redesign the shape of the teams and their capabilities to match the demand of the work that those teams receive. In one example, Waste Detectives found that 20% of the interactions and pain points in a collection of teams was identified to not have a specific engineering resource in place. When the leaders redesigned the team shape to include that engineering capacity, the waste (blockers) reduced and the flow rate of the products increased.

This was achievable due to new-found knowledge of how the teams were blocking each other. Those interactions and pain points can be continuously reduced and removed across the organisation with continual improvements.

As organisations grow, a level of organisational design is embedded and this adapts over a period of time when companies are bought and added, or when parts are divested and sold to create new ones. However, when organisations grow at a rapid pace, they can become so big that, before long, they have multiple competing purposes.

Let's look at one example of this: eBay. The auction site grew so big, it bought a payments tool, PayPal, in 2002. The marriage ended in 2015 after 13 years as it was no longer economically viable for them to be together. They had two different purposes and so they could operate better on their own. The separation agreement had a clause in it that the companies had to adhere to for a period of time. After that, they were totally on their own.

Looking into the future, do you think Amazon products and delivery could split from its AWS Cloud business?

At a certain point in time, any organisation has a particular organisation design in place. But over time, friction points arise which either need to be designed out or adjusted to make them operate effectively.

However, organisations don't always have to separate. In the eBay/PayPal example, the organisation clearly had two purposes and one was holding back the other from growing. For PayPal, it made sense to go it alone and flourish in the world of digital payment services.

All organisations have friction points caused by interactions within the organisation and externally with other organisations or regulators. Each of the interaction, friction points and bottlenecks that constrain the delivery of meaningful products to customers at pace.

Here are some examples of interactions and friction points that the Waste Detective methods allow you to find:

1. **Who**: Team A.
   What: Blocked from delivering iPhone products by third-party supplier Y not providing access to a development environment.
   Impact: Team B cannot deliver the new digital payment method to iphone customers.
   Days Delayed: 10 [Impact Effect High Easy to Fix [HE] (See Chapter 3)
2. **Who**: Team B
   What: Supplier Y unable to provide a test environment until the contract has been agreed and signed.
   Impact: Team C cannot prepare the automation testing scripts.
   Days Delayed : 15
3. **Who**: Digital governance team
   What: The iPhone code deployment needs to be approved by a governance committee, but they do not meet for another 13 days.
   Impact: Team B cannot prepare the automation testing scripts.
   Days Delayed: 12 [Impact Effect High Easy to Fix [HE]

In the examples above, we can see that the digital governance team's infrequent cadences is a friction point to teams trying to release value. The third-party supplier providing the development environment is also causing the pace of delivery to slow. The team has to stop work due to waste.

It won't take you long to gather waste data and accumulate knowledge that allows you to find the interaction, pain and friction points that cause waste and sap capacity.

The Waste Detectives knowledge will provide insight into where the organisation can be improved by putting resources in place to support the demand of work.

When considering organisation redesign, *Team Topologies* by Matthew Skelton and Manuel Pais (2019) covers how teams and organisational design are a work in progress and can be said to adapt over time. Some points that resonate with finding and removing waste are that the approach will not be effective unless the following are in place:

- A healthy culture
- Good engineering practices
- Healthy funding (We touched on Opex and Capex in Chapter 3)
- Clarity of business vision.

Let's address these areas in relation to interaction and pain points when trying to find and remove waste.

ORGANISATIONAL CULTURE

Mindset and wanting to improve the organisation is vital. The leadership culture, from top to bottom, needs to be one of wanting to improve and deliver what the customer wants, without fear. We will explore what happens when this goes wrong with the help of a case study: Nokia.

If you remember the 1990s, you'll remember Nokia. For those of us using phones at the time, this was the go-to phone. It was durable, with long battery life, and almost everyone I knew (including Tony, who didn't want to buy jeans online) had one. But Nokia's culture held it back.

In 1999, Nokia had a profit of $4 billion. In 2007, Apple introduced the iPhone but even then Nokia still had 50% of the market. But over the next 6 years, Nokia lost 90% of its value.

> *"Before the meltdown of mobile valuations in 2001, Nokia's market cap soared to US $260 billion; in August 2002 it was US $54 billion. Although it fared better than most of its rivals, business was no longer about dreams, but about 'making best execution an asset"*
> *— The Mobile Revolution, Dan Stenibock, 2005*

From a customer perspective, the market had started to move towards touch-screen phones. But Nokia was so focused on delivery, it failed to understand what the customer wanted. It fatally overestimated the brand value of Nokia products and didn't innovate. On top of that, it had to contend with destructive internal competition and failed to upgrade to Android software. All these factors saw the demise of a world-leading phone producer in a relatively short period of time.

Nokia failed to see the opportunity of joining the Android journey with competitors such as Samsung, with Android phones being very affordable. Nokia assumed its market dominance would be sufficient, believing that their customers would still want a keypad as opposed to a touch screen. Around this time, I recall going into a phone shop and trying out a few phones. I recall being blown away by the ease of use of the Apple iPhone from a useability perspective, but have since moved to Android due to the lower cost. Android works for me.

Nokia did eventually see the opportunity, but far too late, with the Symbian operating system. But by this time competitors in the form of Apple and Android were far away into the distance in terms of what they could offer customers.

Now far behind Apple and Android, having lost market dominance and lots of money, it made another poor decision. It made a deal with Microsoft, which eventually went on to acquire Nokia. Again on a personal note, I thought I'd try one of these phones, purely down to the cost But as I recall I lasted about two weeks before taking it back to replace it with Apple or Android. This was due to the phone simply being too difficult to use. As a previous customer of Apple i personally had simply become used to a highly usable phone, which unfortunately Nokia failed to achieve.

However, in 2023 Nokia phones are still available and I like what I've read about them online:

- There are Nokia 5G phones that are made from recycled materials, tapping into the sustainability aspect: https://www.nokia.com/phones/en_gb/sustainability
- The phones can be self-repaired, saving money in an economic cycle that is hard on customers' finances: https://www.nokia.com/phones/en_gb/self-repair
- Low-cost models are very appealing considering the current financial difficulties faced by customers.

I am tempted to try Nokia again in the future, just to see what they are like. The sustainable, lost cost and easy to repair phone is something I like the sound of.

SUMMARY:

- Always consider what the customer wants.
- Allow openness, to allow bad messages to be heard.
- Use company resources effectively.
- Hire qualified people

Nokia assumed customers would flock back to them, but it's fair to say that hasn't happened. [20]

Nokia's organisational culture thought its market dominance would prevail but lost sight of the need to innovate and provide what was important to the customer. The company was reluctant to take risks and consider technical advances in the market driven by software. Its leadership couldn't adapt and could be viewed as command and control and dictatorial. Having hit tough times, the leadership needed an adaptive mindset to empower colleagues to innovate and try new ideas. [21]

---

[20] https://startuptalky.com/reasons-why-nokia-failed/
[21] https://predictableprofits.com/where-did-nokia-go-wrong-and-six-lessons-you-can-learn-from-them/

Having command and control leadership can drive the wrong mindset and behaviours. This is linked with the push for financial growth as a focus, but taking an eye off innovation is risky. From the example of Nokia, we can see how this can have a dramatic impact on an organisation. They did have sufficient resources to maintain innovation and develop new ideas, but their focus was on delivery.

Lets now explore the contrast between leaders with a traditional mindset and adaptive leaders who explore positions frequently and change direction and pivot when required.

In a typical organisation with a traditional mindset and leadership behaviours, leaders are not normally aware that their thinking drives how the system of change team or lab operates and ultimately affects performance.

Further reading on Thinking -> System -> Performance in Beyond Command and Control by John Seddon (2019)

Let's say that you are a systems developer who is concentrating on delivering a customer feature to the next product release. The developer is focused and motivated. The leader has just come from a meeting with an action that they want carried out. They ask the developer to drop their task and pick up the new task. What are the consequences to the team/lab performance and morale? The developer has to task-switch and lose focus, so the customer product may not get delivered in that sprint or release cycle. The team and product owner may miss the option to deliver to the customer to gain feedback to improve the product.

Ask the leaders you are working with:

- How many times have you done this or still do this?
- Can you see the impact and consequences of your actions?

If these signs are visible, perhaps you may want to help them stop it.

Let's relate this to mindset. Adaptive leaders realise they have two key jobs:

Job 1 - Deliver meaningful products to customers.
Job 2 - Improve the system: Continuously improve.

Traditional leaders tend to focus on Job 1. They are separated from the work, making decisions on past experience and focusing on keeping busy whilst managing the budget. They are typically just thinking and operating in Job 1 mode.

In contrast, digital minded leaders recognise how mission critical Job is 2, and focus on both Job 1 and Job 2. But they are integrated with the work and understand, or are curious to know, what the customer wants. They can measure the value of the product to what is being consumed and used by the customers related to their ever-changing needs and demands by Objectives and Key Results (OKRs).

OKR's offer a framework to set goals and track the performance of delivering against those goals, when delivering products to customers in an agile method. It looks at alignment of the work being done to the goals, making them visible throughout the organisation.

OKR Reading : [22]

Leaders use knowledge to act on the system of change to make continual improvement. This could be done by understanding what is slowing them down via waste data, through to the value being delivered to the customer.

The leaders also have the ability to use the measurements from the OKRs to gain knowledge of how improvements are being made within the organisation.

What type of leader are you working with?

Let's loop back to Nokia. The company lost sight of what the customer wanted and did not innovate to address what mattered to the customer. Sure, Nokia was exceptional at mass producing good-quality phones. But what mattered to the customer had changed. You might say that Nokia was stuck in Job 1 mode, acting as a traditional organisation.

---

[22] https://kanbanize.com/agile/scaled-agile/okrs-in-agile

To bring this back to finding and removing waste, leaders need knowledge of the interaction and pain points from the teams finding waste. But we need leaders to be fully in Job 2 mode, wanting to continually improve and reduce the friction points caused by waste to deliver value as quickly and efficiently as possible. They can do this by creating experiments to remove it and then teams measuring the results to see if it has improved the flow of products to customers.

So, senior leaders may ask, what's in it for me? Well, tell them that they will get more capacity to deliver and this can make you more competitive.

Are your senior leaders you're working with focused on both Job 1 - Deliver Meaningful Products to Customers and Job 2 - Improve the system?

ENGINEERING PRACTICES

One place to start is to have a look at the number of engineers versus other roles as a percentage across the organisation. The engineers are the ones who create and release code that produces the products your customers want to use. The engineers are the ones that are producing digital measuring products that are consumed by customers. By knowing your flow rates of products to customers and an indication of where work slows due to engineering constraints, hands offs (which can be identified via waste). Were the organisation to have a shortfall of engineers, that could impede flow of digital products to customers.

You need the ability to innovate quickly and on demand, whilst having the capabilities your developers need to deliver products to customers as fast as possible in order to gain valuable feedback.

Adaptive organisations are looking to focus on continuous delivery of meaningful products to customers. Organisations that don't provide good engineering practices, risk a higher churn rate of developers or not being able to attract the right engineers to keep competitive.

FUNDING

Fixed-sized teams with all the types of resources needed to deliver end-to-end features to customers, fully funded in an annual budget cycle, is something that you may be in currently or have seen in the past. The team has the resource types and capacity to deliver regular increments of the product or feature to its customers. The team's delivery of products or features to customers is aligned to OKRs. So the team and the organisation is able to measure value being released to its customers. This allows product owners to have sufficient resources and not to worry about how the team is funded and paid for throughout that budget cycle.

Teams that are not fully funded, that require ad hoc inbound work commitments to be able to pay for the resources in the team, often struggle on which work item to deliver next. Their priority may be skewed to whoever is paying for the work to fund the team, as opposed to the most valuable piece of work for the customer and the organisation. Alternatively, they start to take on more work to secure funding for another few quarters, only to stack up problems of uncompleted work.

Now let's look at the potential consequence of this when waste is observed in a lab or team. The Waste Detectives Methods may have been used to spot an interaction or pain point having to hand off work to another resource in another team. The situation was created by the limitations of the funding model at the start of the cycle. The team had a demand to deliver but this resource is outside of their budgetary control for 12 months. The rate of products to customers slows, but due to budget constraints, the senior leadership was unable to draw down any further funding. Or, the rigidity of the organisation did not allow the product owner to reorganise the capacity based on the demand needed to deliver the products.

Leaders and product owners need the ability to adapt the team shape and size according to the demands of the customers. To achieve this, teams need the resources to deliver those demands and get value release back on track with the measurable goal of pace of delivery and value to customer, as well as fast feedback. However, traditional leaders are fixated on managing budgets, and not value release.

An example of this could be if the team is fully funded but the waste knowledge has identified a need for a specific development resource in another area. The lack of access to this resource is sapping the ability for this team to deliver at pace.

What would help a product owner or engineering lead is to have access to funding to re-shape the team to how they see fit, based on the knowledge they have gained, to improve the performance of the team or lab.

Consider a funding model that allows the teams to flex the demand and provide some empowerment over the budget to the product owner.

In the example above, team morale would drop as they cannot deliver products and they have identified the pain points. But they are unable to act, due to a constrained funding model. Fixed-funding models can also affect innovation. Where the teams are able to access skills from other areas in the organisation to test and learn, the ability to adapt and make resources available for improvements can have an impact.

Many years ago, I worked at a software company in which one area was doing well and was innovating, with clients coming back for more and more products. Another area was in trouble, so they had to stop innovation and focus on delivery to cover costs. In the end, it almost brought down both areas of the business, due to the client not being able to get what they wanted.

A focus on innovation keeps you fresh, just as the sudden ability to buy jeans online brought customers' actual needs sharply into focus.

Having looked at funding, now let's move on to vision and purpose.

VISION / PURPOSE

Let's reflect on Nokia's purpose. It is: "At Nokia, we create technology that helps the world act together." Relating your purpose to the products and services is essential to measure how you are delivering, and Nokia certainly delivered a lot of phones.

In contrast, Apple's purpose is: "We build products to empower everyone."

They are different words, but "helping the world act together" sounds like it could be a video call on WhatsApp or using a banking app to make a payment.

The vision / purpose focuses senior l leaders and the whole organisation on what it is trying to achieve for the customer. Having defined the purpose, the organisation can measure key results linked back to the purpose via OKRs. [23]

The Waste Detectives method can help you show what is preventing the organisation from delivering value at pace. To achieve the purpose, you can pull in the knowledge of the interaction or pain points. This will help you know where the pace of delivery of capacity is being sapped.

In a perfect world, you'd have an organisation design that worked really well, with few or no friction points and constraints to the flow of meaningful products to customers. However, team members leave and arrive, product direction changes, technology moves quickly, and customer demands change. So organisation change over time is essential.

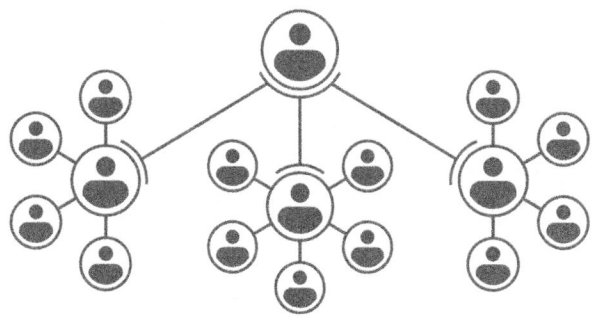

Figure 7.1: Organisational Design
Image by Menara Grafis / Shutterstock.com

---

[23] https://kanbanize.com/agile/scaled-agile/okrs-in-agile

By having a design in place, an organisation allows teams to work together, passing items of dependent work items such as user stories through a series of teams that are dependent on one another to deliver meaningful products at pace to its customers. With the aid of PI Planning the teams' and labs' work can be sequenced and the dependencies recorded between the epics and user stories. In theory, at this point, as we have logged the dependencies of who needs what from each team, the work will flow. When something is needed from another team at a certain point, the customer value will simply flow out on time. [24]

In reality, this is not always the case. Impediments can have an impact on these dependencies, causing pain points.

> *"Well-defined interactions help make effective teams, this is especially true for remote work situations."*
>
> —Matthew Skelton and Manuel Pais, RemoteTeams Interactions Workbook, 2022[25]

Now let's explore a huge change that impacted organisations back in 2020.

The Covid-19 pandemic brought about a dramatic sea-change in how organisations operated. The 9 to 5, five-days-a-week in an office organisational operating model changed overnight, with many transformational change colleagues working from home. Many are still doing this, with the occasional collaboration day spent in the office when required.

Many transformation programmes are now moving to an adaptive and agile environment with a number of agile coaches and change consultants. Work is now distributed to a number of teams, tribes and labs as interconnecting parts in the organisation design. The design has

---

[24] https://www.scaledagileframework.com/pi-planning/,
[25] https://www.scaledagileframework.com/pi-planning/,

typically been put in place by a senior leadership team which may or may not have been supported by a consultancy company.

In *Remote Teams Interactions Workbook*, Matthew Skelton and Manuel Pais explains that, "Some dependencies might be fine today, but in a few months' time they will be slowing down the dependent team too much and you'll need to address it." Your organisation could have hundreds or thousands of interconnections and dependencies that could cause friction points and pain to the organisation.

8.1

We looked at methods to find where the waste was slowing down the work. This waste knowledge it captures allows you to see how the interactions between parts of the organisation have friction points and to measure the impact of these friction points. The information on these waste friction points is the view of the dependencies between teams throughout the organisation and how it impacts the pace of products delivered to your customers.

Dependencies are built into the alignment of the work from PI planning between the teams. The work is sequenced to allow the best possible chance of achieving the outcome.

In a traditional way of working, when a team had a commitment to deliver something that needed work from another team and there was a problem identified, this would typically be managed via a risk management method. Raising a risk or issue typically follows a set format, which in some cases could be as follows (shown in Table 4.1):

Table 7.1. Risk Management

Topic	Description
Impact	What is the impact of the risk or issue to the work or customer if this risk or issue were to arise? This could be a time delay, additional costs, reputational damage or impact on other works associated with, or dependent on, this piece of work.

Assessment	Assessing the risk or issue to gather more information and understand it better to help us understand the consequences if it happens. This might involve a number of individuals from specialist areas related to the work. Then the person assessing the risk looks at the probability of the risk actually happening.
Mitigation	The set of works or activities that would need to happen to resolve the risk or issue. This allows you to have a way of mitigating the risk if this happens. It could also mean having funding set aside that can be drawn down by the feature teams or labs when needed.
Probability	The likelihood of the risk materialising or happening. It could be as simple as a High, Medium or Low, or using a formula specific to the company or business management team to order the risk in terms of the chances of it happening.

I - Impact
A - Assess
M - Mitigation
P - Probability

However, tracking and reporting where you have a problem **doesn't help** the work progress towards the customers. It doesn't allow the leadership team to see what is happening in the organisation design to understand why these issues and risks are happening to slow product delivery to customers.

However, when you ask a traditional leader, "Where are your interactions and pain points?" their default position may be to tell you the risks and issues and dependencies straight out of their project management playbook.

As a CTO the aim is to get the senior leaders you are working with to make decisions based on knowledge, so they become more adaptive leaders.

Looking back and assessing risks is not being a digital leader in the work and acting on knowledge. There will be some higher-level risks that may need this, but if you have pain points in the work, you could be losing a large percentage of capacity every day and your risks are just being talked about by business management. Get into the work and see where your hand-offs are not working effectively. As CTO, you want to get the senior l leaders you are working with into the work, and tweak the organisational design via experimentation.

The organisational design is potentially not working in places and the waste will be able to show those interactions and pain points. This will allow a redesign of the teams to allow the work to flow more smoothly. This means higher capacity for the organisation. But in order to achieve this in consultation with your digital leaders, you'll need to focus on continuous improvement as well as delivery, potentially working 50:50 on these two aspects.

In order to understand the different team shapes, read *Team Topologies* by Matthew Skelton and Manuel Pais, 2019.

DEPENDENCIES IDENTIFIED FROM WASTE DETECTING

We discussed aligning the work through techniques such as Programme Increment (PI)
planning earlier in this chapter. Coming out of Programme Increment (PI) planning, dependencies will be interlocked between areas such as value streams / labs and teams. This could be at a portfolio level and quite some distance from the actual work. This would assume that this process is complete, however the Programme Increment (PI) may not be fully connected and aligned to the teams actually doing the work. When the lower level teams plan and break down the work further, then the teams and labs start to know the full needs of one and other via interactions. Where these interactions are not effective, they would be identified as blockers via The Waste Detectives Methods. [26]

We looked at knowledge on what is blocking the work. Some of these could be "routine" reasons for work to be blocked, which may identify where a particular resource is not available within a particular

---

[26] https://www.scaledagileframework.com/pi-planning/#:~:text=Program%20Increment%20(PI)%20Planning%20is,you%20are%20not%20doing%20SAFe

feature team. Two experts referred to this as follows, with Deming like Shewhart's earlier works. [27]

1. Walter Shewhart referred to "routine" causes.
2. W.E. Deming referred to these as "common causes".

W. Edwards Deming (1982), *Out of the Crisis*;
These have an impact on the flow of work to customers and can impact the service level expectation and the probabilistic forecasting of delivery of products to customers as used in approaches such as ProKanban. [28]

These common causes that you'll gain from The Waste Detectives' methods could potentially allow you to see where a team is not working with another team or a third party is not operating effectively. The flow of work and the time work takes to deliver is typically longer, so this provides an opportunity to redesign the organisation. Depending on the work, this could involve moving resource capability into the team, thus removing the dependency that was causing the blocker (waste).

For further reading on kanban and "routine" and "common causes". [29]

The following exercises will allow teams and labs to start grouping waste by system conditions and themes, then go on to consider common causes of waste.

EXERCISE A - THEMES OF WASTE

This is a high-level exercise which you can do with teams to show the high-level interaction and pain points within a team or lab to generate curiosity about what is slowing down the pace of delivery.

---

[27] https://www.leansixsigmadefinition.com/glossary/walter-shewhart/
[28] https://prokanban.org/
[29] https://prokanban.org/

1. Pick a feature team or lab
2. Hold a workshop session with the team virtually or in a room
3. Ask the team / lab: What is stopping us from delivering?
   a. Capture the information on the wall: "These are known as system conditions"
   b. Group this information into themes
4. Ask the team or lab: what is the impact of what is stopping us?
   a. Align this to the system conditions and themes
5. Build a diagram to show system conditions and themes and what this drives within the teams/labs.

Other outputs from this type of session could draw a diagram that shows how teams need other teams to deliver (team-to-team dependency) with the pain points overlaid.

Example: Write the team names in bubbles. Where a team needs another team to deliver, draw a line to connect the teams. Where you have waste or delay data add the interaction and pain points to the diagram.

Note: You could expand this activity to build a business diagram of how the organisation interacts with the following perspectives:

- Team-to-team relations.
- Team to third party organisations.

A secondary exercise could be to add the waste knowledge found in chapter 3 and value via the OKRs over the top. This would help you visualise any interaction pain points that exist and identify areas to experiment and improve.

EXERCISE B

With your teams/labs or value stream, pull out a few control charts or scatter plots from the flow data and have a look for the outliers.

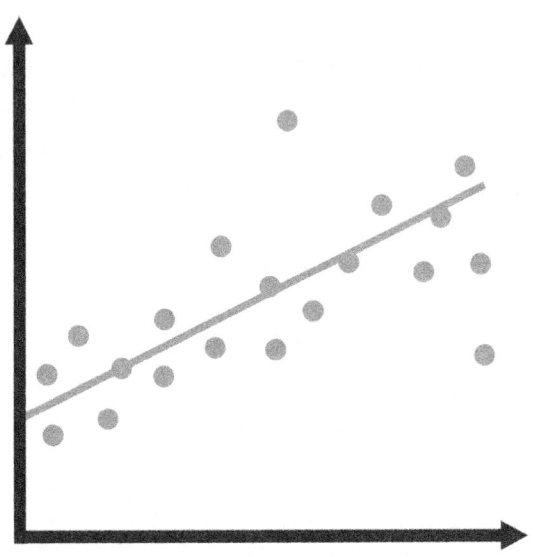

Figure 7.2: Scatter Plot
Image by Mari-Leaf / Shutterstock.com

These will be the dots towards the top of the chart; an indication that something "exceptional" happened at that point that caused pain or friction in the flow of work of products to customers. You might have heard other names for this from the works of W.E. Deming and Walter Shewhart. Deming referred to these as "special causes" and Shewhart as "assignable causes."

Gather the following information in these pieces of work:

- What was the "exceptional" cause for this work to take longer?
- What was the impact on flow?

- Are there any mitigations needed to reduce the risk of these events preventing the flow of products to customers in the future?
- Remember, an outlier may not be really exceptional. There may not be a special cause reason for it. It could well be part of a common cause variation, part of the systems natural ups and downs, unless you know the reason that makes it exceptional. Senior leaders often dismiss long delays as special causes when they are a natural product of what they manage, This is one of the reasons they can be resistant to the Waste Detectives message.

HOW A CTO CAN USE THESE TECHNIQUES

The organisation design may have been in place prior to you joining the company as CTO. In many organisations the organisation design setup may not be effective, but without knowledge you have no way of knowing. Not knowing if the organisation design is efficient or effective is not a great place to be. As a CTO you want to know how much capacity is used to deliver value and how much capacity is wasted.

The Waste Detectives Methods will allow, through knowledge waste (data) to show where interaction and friction points exist between value streams, labs and teams. Then as a CTO you have a choice to make, live with the capacity being sapped or influence the whole organisation to want to continuously improve and reshape to meet the demand of work flowing through to customers.

By influence and having adaptive leaders with the waste detectives method you can increase capacity to deliver faster to customers.

PRACTICAL STORY

Working with a senior leader for a number of years and introducing the concept of waste detecting to them, this leader had upskilled themselves in adaptive leadership and had a true hunger for knowledge to continuously improve the flow of products to customers. This leader took it upon herself to do both Job 1 and Job 2 to deliver and continuously improve the functions she was leading.

The results of having a leader showing that finding and removing waste made a real difference to the whole function, this brought the whole area together in wanting to improve how the work is delivered and to maximise the capacity to increase flow.

SUMMARY

Job 1 and Job 2 are equally important. Where senior leaders are just focused on delivery and show little to no interest in improving how work is delivered, it could mean that you do not have the right leadership behaviours in place.

The interaction and pain points (waste) will exist everywhere, but how often are leaders within your organisations experimenting to find and remove them?

Managing dependencies and discussing risks and issues for leadership at a higher level. Business Management and leaders typically use this as management information and reporting.

This dependency management mindset isn't getting the leaders into the work and seeing and knowing how it all aligns to deliver value. Knowing the interaction and pain points in the work with the teams is a great way for leaders to understand how they can get started and be in the work, as true leaders do (Job 2).

How to

Find out how the organisation you're working with interacts at a value stream <-> value stream, lab <-> lab, team <-> team and team <-> third party. Then identify where the pain points (waste) exist.

> **TAKEAWAYS**
>
> ⇨ Organisations have many internal and external interdependencies.
> ⇨ Internal and external dependencies and team setups evolve over time.
> ⇨ Dependencies and handoffs that are not effective generate waste and lost capacity.
> ⇨ Digital leaders' work is evenly split between continuous improvement in the work and delivery.
> ⇨ Digital minded leaders need to be in the work and understand how the organisation works and where the problems are.

CHAPTER 8

CONNECTING ALL PARTS OF THE CHANGE AREA ON THE JOURNEY

THE ORGANISATION IS LIKELY TO HAVE many teams involved in the end to end delivery of products to customers. Therefore, the finding and removal of waste has to happen at the same level - across many teams. There will be many types of teams involved with the delivery of value to customers. In order to achieve the goal of increasing capacity and delivering products to customers quicker with less waste in the system. As a CTO, trying to connect all these many teams together so everyone is on the same page and removing waste is going to benefit the organisation as a whole.

This chapter covers form techniques to aid connecting all the parts, but also looks at the resilience needed.

KEY CONCEPTS

In order to find and remove waste in an organisation on a full-scale transformation journey, you are going to need to include many parts of the organisation in the journey. Connected parts of the organisation will need to buy into the transformational philosophy of trying to embed removing waste at scale. In order to get continued improvement methodology in order to increase capacity and the pace and flow rate of meaningful products to customers.

In a traditional large-scale organisation delivering change, there are going to be many different pockets of expertise and suppliers that enable the organisation to perform.

Standing back and thinking about this, it may seem a bit overwhelming and perhaps something like the diagram below. As a digital leader you want each of those areas to be curious.

Figure 8.1: Connecting All Parts
Image by Funtap / Shutterstock.com

The areas you may have to influence and connect together could be, but are not limited to:

- Scrum master - Communities
- Product owner - Communities
- Engineering - Communities
- Third-party suppliers
- Contract management
- Capability and training

- Business analysis - Communities
- Project and programme management - Communities
- Testing / Quality assurance - Communities
- Production release
- Change directors and technical directors
- Agile coaching / System thinking

Going all in and covering the bases would involve a massive effort and something to consider is that each person or area will need to come on the journey at the pace they are ready to accept change and adapt their ways of working to finding and removing waste. On my journey, I started small and grew the concept organically, increasing the levels and circle of influence bit by bit until enabling the concept as something that was strategically important. Proving the concept and getting buy-in along the way was by no means plain sailing. Expect to have to draw on your drive and resilience.

Remember Tony and his views on buying jeans online? He wasn't convinced and you are going to meet many Tonys along the way.

POSSIBLE JOURNEY TO CONNECT THE ORGANISATION PARTS

Stage 1 - Start Small to Prove it Works

Finding and removing waste starts with the concept and then grows and expands, similar to an oak tree growing from an acorn. But hopefully, with a fair wind and this book, you will embed the finding and removal of waste quicker than growing a tree!.

First find one or two teams with scrum masters and product owners that have digital leader characteristics. Work with the scrum masters and product owners and team members, and be open about what you are trying to achieve. Get into the work and learn learn learn: what the data is telling the whole team.

An initial concept I tried with a team was to limit work-in-progress (WIP) to one user story per person in a 'Swim Lane' kanban method. We all planned the work together then pulled the work into the kanban, only for a developer to block a piece of work straight away. "I'm blocked and I'm not going to do any work," he said with a smile on his face. The culture of the company was bad and its leadership didn't want to remove waste. The developer wanted to carry on multitasking and was happy for work to be blocked and did not want to be curious and try something new. It's very similar to Tony not wanting to buy jeans online.

No one reacted, we just took it as learning. To have the developer believing that this was going to make a difference, we needed to demonstrate that there was a willingness to fix the problems being encountered. We needed to show that there was a focus on making things better over time. The core belief was that we would get there.

In the next six to twelve months, the flow rate to the customer had doubled and had removed half of the waste (blockers) that prevented the work being delivered. In other words, the engineer was now metaphorically in the frame of mind to buy jeans online. But this was just one encounter and one engineer!

Consider an organisation with thousands, if not tens of thousands, of developers and change professionals. One at a time is going to be too slow. But proving the concept of finding and removing waste in one area will start to grow curiosity and belief. Those using it will learn how the approach works and feels.

Stage 1 is now complete. Expect the Tonys not wanting to buy jeans online to smile, wave and carry on. Expect them to ignore the method and its adoption about them.

Stage 2 - Expand the Team Usage

Now you have proven the concept in one team, look to expand to maybe three or five more teams in the same area as the first, or elsewhere depending on what you need to learn. Just because the first team came on board, it may not be as easy with the next batch of teams. You carefully selected the first team by choosing people with the right behaviours, mindset and characteristics as digital leaders.

So now, have a session with all those in the work and try to include leaders and decision makers from the business side of the fence as well as those delivering change via the transformation teams. Just because it worked once doesn't mean it will work again.

Expanding to more teams gains more knowledge but also more resistance. In my experience, some of the teams wanted a bespoke method for capturing and removing waste. This can pose a threat to the overall vision of finding and removing waste for the organisation. To understand and act on knowledge to enable leaders across an entire organisation, data-led decision making and having bespoke solutions all over the place just isn't going to work.

Listen, learn and prototype to start with. Make decisions and always keep your eye on the prize. Objections along the lines of, "Can we do it this way or this way?" will grow and grow. So will your need and willingness to pick the best ideas, embed them into the design, and say "No" again and again where necessary to make it happen.

Many teams will work well and help the influencing. One or two may not be ready for such a new concept. Try and help them because momentum really helps a large-scale rollout.

But at this stage, the outcome has been achieved. The concept of removing waste and increasing flow has been proven across a handful of teams.

Stage 2 is now complete. A few more Tonys are identified, but the journey is still progressing.

Stage 3 - Lab and Value Stream Leaders

This is an interesting stage. You have now potentially shown that teams have removed waste and increased the pace of delivery of products to the customers. You may be feeling proud of the method and what the teams have achieved. You have all collaborated and it has worked and made a real difference to those in the work.

Now in an organisation with adaptive leadership embedded, you can expect them to be curious and want to get into the work and possibly give it a go. But in a traditional organisation at the start or mid-way through its transformation journey with command and control leaders embedded, you can expect to meet Tonys on steroids. My first encounter with a number of leaders had one person say, "Wow this stuff is gold dust!" and nine others dismissing the idea as nonsense. They ignored it, discrediting the concept.

But again, treat all this as learning. The leaders are not in the work and do not want to be in the work. Some of the teams said, "So we are doing all of this, where are the leaders?" This is referred to as the frozen middle, where at the top you want to embed it, and at the bottom the teams are doing it.

Try to get the leaders into the work, whilst at the same time opening up a second or third front. Find new value streams: agile coaches, product owners, scrum masters and go again and again. Over time, the groundswell of data and waste being identified will start to build the knowledge about the amount of waste and capacity being sapped by the organisation. Where possible, write them up into case studies and make them available across the whole of the organisation. This will increase the pull from those who are curious, the ones who are potentially your leaders of the future, to replace the traditional leaders.

Stage 4 - Putting it on the Strategic Agenda

Getting The Waste Detectives Methods on the strategic agenda, in the long term could involve many or not all parts of the organisation. So increasing the amount of curiosity and willingness and wanting to go after the problem to find and remove waste, should help the strategic aspect.

But unless an innovative idea of embedding, finding and removing waste has backing and ownership and accountability at the top table, there is always a risk that all the hard work and focus can come undone.

Now if you were a consultancy company, you'd have the ears of the people at the top and would be able to influence at a higher level to start with. But you would then need to cover the steps in chapter 1 to gain buy-in at the coal face and upwards to embed a method that works and delivers empowerment and ownership across the whole organisation.

However, you are a CTO and so getting time with a change or transformation director at the very top of an organisation is going to be tricky. You are going to need to show and tell, influence, and keep widening the network across the organisation, trying to find a line or connection into the change or transformation director. Find supporters and others who want to improve the business with the same or similar agenda to your own.

When you do find those connections, remember that people at the very top are spinning lots of plates. They have also seen ideas come and go and consultants come and go, so why would you be any different to any others that have come in and failed in the past?

You know your concept is equivalent to the Apple iPhone, but they may think that finding and removing waste is a BlackBerry. Try and get the leadership curious and at that point you can start to explore the modifying of language from waste (blockers) at a lab and team level to the opportunity at large. And, more importantly, the problem you are helping them solve.

LANGUAGE

Swap your language to talk about "opportunity", and, "a problem we can solve for you" so it switches to what's in it for them.

Listen to the language during the conversations. Be clear what you want to achieve as an outcome from the session. This concept is new and innovative so it may make some individuals feel vulnerable about their lack of knowledge. Remember how Tony felt about buying jeans online? Reflectors need time to digest and get a sense of what or how this can be a game changer to make them better as change directors and transformation directors.

Note: You may see dismissive behaviour if leaders feel vulnerable, just note it as this point. Your journey will just take a little longer. Keep having the conversations.

One concept they may be thinking of if you get buy-in, is how do they influence their leaders to make this happen with the right behaviours across the organisation? Hopefully, the organisation has good digital minded leaders in place.

RESILIENCE AND PUTTING YOUR ARMOUR BACK ON

The Tonys you encounter will sap your energy again and again, so finding a mechanism to put your armour on and re-energise helps you survive the marathon that embedding the finding and removal of waste is going to be. For me, this is getting in the sea with a board and having the wetsuit on but you'll have your own way of dealing with it mentally.

I felt shattered at times: broken, like the armour was being stripped off me left, right and centre. This at times left me dysfunctional, unhappy and ineffective due to the sheer amount of resistance that just kept coming. I would describe this phrase as getting over the mound to embed and influence the whole organisation.

The unhappiness this can cause is described in *The Broken CEO* by Chris Pearse. You may experience one or more of the following:

- The Worrier
- The Imposter
- The Victim
- The Casualty
- The Blamer
- The Pauper
- The Miserable Millionaire
- The Misfit
- The People Pleaser

Chris Pearse's book relates to CEOs but reflecting on myself, I put myself in the "Misfit" category of having thoughts that just don't fit. Looking back, this wasn't really the case, just that the product thinking and vision was so far ahead of the organisational pace of embedding it. It's like waiting for everyone else to catch up. These are just emotions and feelings to watch out for; leading the delivery of new concepts can be a solo effort for a while.

Stay fixed to the purpose and use measures to align back to the purpose when you have particularly tricky individuals. Listen to them, but never forget their behaviour. As you grow your team on the journey, delegate and trust those individuals to have a go. You are all going after the same problem to try to resolve it.

Not all resistance is in the open. Some of it is covert and behind the scenes. As the concepts develop pace and recognition, the "People Pleasers" will swoop in and try to kick you off the ball and promote the idea and concept as their own. This only lasts for a brief period as they do not have the knowledge, vision and knowhow to make it happen. Stick to your guns and be strong on your mission.

The ability to influence and stay resilient comes down to your own behaviours. Some good principles on this come from Dale Carnegie in *How To Win Friends and Influence People*:

1. Do not criticise, condemn or complain
2. Give honest and sincere appreciation

Listen and be curious about what someone is telling you, practise active listening and be eager to know how others think and feel. The longer you are on the journey, the more times you will meet similar types of people, so test and learn their responses and interactions. Try to influence them in certain ways. Reflect on how it went and if it works try it again, if not change and go again.

Being authentic and listening and considering all views is the best way of building and embedding a great new way of working. When it's over the mound and starting to embed, it's a pleasure to hear all the stories about how they are using the Waste Detectives' method.

Keep in mind that It is definitely worth it as the Tonys pop up. Smile, wave and carry on with the journey.

SELL AND LISTEN

Having had some success, it's time to sell sell sell and get the whole organisation curious about finding and removing waste. Start leveraging the digital age: podcasts, vlogs, chat rooms. The more people you can reach, the better, and monitor the Tony messages coming back. Some of them will be valid and may require an intervention or adjustment along the way. This isn't command and control, it's about collaborating and embedding this across the organisation.

Engage with all the areas in the business with lunch and learns, presentations and discussions. Be open and reach out to all the areas:

EXERCISE

1. Work with a scrum master, product owner and team.
2. Find and Remove Waste using The Waste Detectives Methods.
3. Produce and distribute a podcast on how it went:
   a. Waste found
   b. How it felt for the team
   c. Lessons learnt.
   d. Gain feedback and knowledge

Building up a series of podcasts of the journey from lots of different perspectives on how it felt as well as whether or not it worked useful. To find and remove waste, it's not just about delivery of a method, it's about taking everyone on the journey with you. All perspectives are useful and valuable as well as knowing how everyone is feeling (and felt) along the way. There are always lessons to learn in order to make it better as you scale the method.

HOW A CTO CAN USE THESE TECHNIQUES

By working with your agile coaches and scrum masters, you can use these techniques to encourage them to start small with a number of teams and then organically grow the method and build the usage of The Waste Detectives Methods across the organisation.

The agile coaches and scrum masters building the method and capabilities into the teams will face resistance at times. This could affect their resilience and I'd recommend having some form of resilience training to support these individuals.

PRACTICAL STORY

When introducing The Waste Detectives Methods into new areas, I work using The Waste Detectives Methods I typically start with one or two teams and go through the learning to show the value of capturing waste, taking it 1 step at a time. Then within a short period of time the waste and friction and pain points start to expose themselves, then bring in the senior leaders. Who more often than not are looking to scale the approach and access the rest of the teams.

The more the method is used, the more resistance falls away and then disappears.

SUMMARY

Start small and gain knowledge and learnings about how it's working and how it feels. Scale into a number of other teams and gain more knowledge; adapt if needed. The more you scale, the more waste you'll find in the value stream, lab and team. Engage with every area and take them all on the journey.

As you speak to people higher up the organisation, soften your language from talking about waste and problems to the opportunity of delivering more valuable products to customers at increased rate of flow due to freeing up capacity. Remember to focus on the future and opportunity, otherwise they will be defensive and feel judged on the historic record you are seen to be exposing.

Leverage how the change or transformation directors can encourage the middle-layer managers to come on board as they'll need some encouragement.

Even when you receive negative vibes, believe in the approach. The reward of seeing the finding and removal of waste embedded is worth it.

TAKEAWAYS

⇨ Start small and prove the concept.
⇨ Grow to a small number of teams.
⇨ Open a second or third font and grow more and more teams.
⇨ Pull in scrum masters to help you, who have digital leader characteristics.
⇨ Expect resistance at all levels; the higher up in the organisation the greater the potential resistance.
⇨ Sell and keep listening; you never know where the next best idea may come from.
⇨ Overcome resistance, but learn from it.
⇨ Change the language from problem to opportunity when required.

CHAPTER 9
PRODUCT MANAGEMENT

THROUGHOUT THE BOOK WE HAVE BEEN discussing senior leadership, embedding the method and capabilities and making decisions to remove waste to improve flow. By building a knowledge repository of waste, establishing ways of working to enable the capturing of data. This chapter looks at concepts for, building this method into an internal product within your organisation to find and remove waste.

It covers the role of a product manager and explores the outcome of a product to find and remove waste.

KEY CONCEPTS

Why are we starting to think of product management in our discussion of finding and removing waste? To explore that, we cover the basis of a method for finding waste in an agile transformation journey, then explore a waste knowledge repository. However, to scale the concept across an organisation, you'll need not only a waste capture method but a knowledge repository, vlogs, podcasts, case

[157]

studies, training materials, example sites and communities to support the implementation at scale.

So let's look at product management and the concepts that could assist you within the organisation you are working with. Finding and removing waste within an organisation will require someone to own the product management. This could be you as CTO kickstarting the initiative, but over time it would potentially need to transition to a set of agile coaches and scrum masters or team to build, maintain and enhance the Waste Detective method being embedded into the organisation.

PRODUCT MANAGER

"The real role of the product manager in the organisation is to work with a team to create the right product that balances meeting business needs with solving user problems" [30]

Now let's explore that quote from our perspective :

Problem we are trying to solve:

- Potentially 50-70% of capacity is being lost to waste.
- Product to customer time is slower than it could be due to waste in the system.
- Capacity and money isn't being used as efficiently as it could be.

Business needs:

- Be clear what the current value is.
- Utilise as much capacity on value work.
- Have as few friction (pain) points as possible.

---

[30] Escaping the Build Trap, Melissa Perri (2019)

Fig. 9.1 : Product Management
Image by Irina Strelnikova / Shutterstock.com

GOOD PRODUCT MANAGER CHARACTERISTICS

Product managers are required to wear many hats, and the word manager isn't related to that of a manager of people.

Product managers need to understand the following:

- Product market
- Business operations
- Purpose / goal of the organisation
- View of the customer that includes empathy
- Influencing

Product managers don't control how things are done and the way that they do them, but more of the "why" the product is being built and the vision and purpose of the product. They define in and validate features or requirements from the surrounding teams and ensure that they stay aligned to the goal and vision.

They need a long-term, entrepreneurial view of what is required, and also a view of what needs to be built, in an experimental way, now. This is because at the start there will be a number of unknowns. Then, over time, they'll need to connect the dots to know what's required when, and how the product can be built and rolled out to customers.

Product managers are building knowledge and learning on how the experiments have worked, joining the dots towards building a product backlog. Then managing products and features for the waste detectives product.

They also need to know what is possible technically versus what the market/customers are expecting.

POOR PRODUCT MANAGER CHARACTERISTICS

To avoid disappointment, let's look at a few characteristics of poor product managers so we know what to avoid.

Project managers moved into product owner roles

A project manager is not the same as being a product owner. Project managers can have command and control behaviours, focusing on keeping resources busy, and wanting to know when the work will get done. They are focused on managing a plan and budgets to ensure the plan gets delivered on time.

Product Managers are operating in a different space, being in the customers' heads and understanding "why" the customer wants the product and "how" they are going to use it.

Some project management activities are needed but these can be picked up by those doing the work, possibly in the agile space, using methodologies such as Kanban.

When organisations go through a transformation programme, the need and use of project manager skills diminishes. I have seen organisations relabel the roles of these individuals into product owners or product managers, which I find very surprising as the skillset is not focussed on the "why" for the customer. Those with skills of learning what the customers need, being available to the development team and understanding the customer market make good product owners or product managers, with the project managers being let go or put into planning roles as far away from the products as possible.

Order taker

These people simply go out to the customers and ask them what they want and build a list of requirements. They are simply order takers without any view of the purpose / vision or goal for the product they own. Prioritisation can be difficult. What would you do in this scenario if two customers asked for conflicting things?

EXPLORING THE FINDING AND REMOVAL OF WASTE PROBLEM

A product manager is focused on delivering the outcome required for the customer. How the product is delivered could be via a methodology such as kanban. kanban is a good way for the product manager to know the Service Level Expectation (SLE) or the probabilistic forecast. This allows the teams delivering for the product manager to be able to answer questions from a product owner such as :

- How many of the new product features will be done by a given date?
- What date will a particular feature be delivered?

Additional Reading on kanban can be found at ProKanban.org [31]

As a product owner of finding and removing waste, you'll need to own the product, break down the work needed into the next manageable items, be able to prioritise the work, and have a clear view of the vision and purpose.

---

[31] ProKanban.org

GAPS

Stephen Bundy, author of *The Knowledge Gap*, found that many companies with a strategic plan did not always achieve their strategic goals. This was down to three gaps within the organisation:

- Knowledge gap
- Alignment gap
- Effects gap

Let's explore these gaps through the eyes of a product manager responsible for finding and removing waste. The company's strategy is to deliver meaningful products to customers as fast as possible with the least amount of waste in the system of change.

KNOWLEDGE GAP

Leaders know there is a problem, but typically ask for more and more information down through the organisation. As a digital leader, you need sufficient information to be able to act on it and make a decision.

In terms of finding and removing waste, you are aware that 50-70% of your capacity is potentially being lost to waste but all your reporting is saying that risks are being managed and projects are within budget. Resources are being kept busy. But in reality, they are not working on the right work to deliver meaningful products quickly. With everything seeming to be fine, you ask for more and more information. But as the organisation has operated in the same way for years, you just hear about risks, issues and budgets.

The terms flow, value and waste are alien to leaders and their reports. When asking for waste information, you may get rows and rows of raw data showing the number of days delay and capacity lost. But unfortunately, they don't understand the data. They have hired experts in the field who present the data back and the numbers are shocking. One person I spoke to expressed disbelief and told me not to quote the numbers to anyone. My gut reaction was that this person needed to be put out to pasture as they lacked curiosity in how to understand the knowledge and improve the business.

However, traditional leaders are so focused on delivery that they are unaware that they also have a second job; that of improving ways of working.

These leaders need to adapt, but they are either struggling to adapt or cannot adapt. They show a lack of alignment to what the organisation is trying to achieve and they don't trust those with the capacity to improve it.

ALIGNMENT GAP

The alignment gap is the difference between what the company wants them to do and what they actually do. Now, telling colleagues what to do is demotivating. This can happen when organisations bring in consultants who propose a set way of doing things.

When it comes to finding and removing waste, the goal is to waste knowledge and act on it. But this approach recognises that all organisations are different. Building the waste categories, themes and management information in collaboration with the whole organisation will help to bring everyone together on the journey.

The best way forward is to set an organisational goal with the guiding principles of wanting to find and remove waste. Then work out how decisions can be made from the data at all levels where the information is trusted and acted upon.

EFFECTS GAP

The waste has been found to be 50-70% and as an organisation you want to reduce this waste level to 20-40% through the organisation. Allowing the capabilities to embed and the method scale should allow the waste % reduce and the flow of products to customers increase.

However if leaders were to introduce new governance or adding reporting or controls, this could have an impact on the effect of what is trying to be achieved by finding and removing waste.

The effect could be that you have found waste but not removed any or as much as you had hoped.

FRAMEWORK AND DEPLOYMENT

To solve the problem of finding and removing waste, you'll need to start to think about who will lead this for you. Who will be your Waste Detective, plus who will form a team and support arrangements around them to allow them to operate throughout the organisation. A senior sponsor is a good thing to have and if you can get one, I would thoroughly recommend it. It's nice to let them have a bit of skin in the game as well.

A way to start could be to ask the product owners: how are you currently gaining knowledge of waste in your value stream, lab and teams? Don't be shocked if they don't have anything. Such conversations can show that the work of improving the flow of products to customers via removing waste isn't aligned throughout the organisation. The teams are probably in reactive mode to blockers and waste rather than seeing this as an opportunity to gather knowledge and act on it.

We mentioned giving your sponsor some skin in the game. This comes down to setting the right goals and then having measures around those goals.

In *Escaping the Build Trap*, the author covers this topic in great way and table 9.1, shows what this might mean for you as Waste Detectives.

Purpose	Where do we want to be with finding and removing waste in 2-3 years?	Reduce waste from X% to Y% of the organisations capacity
Outcome	What **Challenges** and **obstacles** are in the way of achieving the vision?	Resistance or scepticism of Customer journey / Value stream leaders
Waste Detective Initiative	What **problems** do we need to solve in order to deliver the product of finding and removing waste?	Creating a team to promote and coordinate the work of finding and removing waste team
Solutions	What solutions, whether tactical or strategic, resolve the problems associated with finding and removing waste?	Finding and removing waste development team

Table 9.1 Purpose / Outcome / Initiative & Solutions
(from *Escaping the Build Trap*, Page 75)

VISION

Setting a long-term vision or purpose aids the alignment and focus that allows the organisation to remove waste at scale. The CTO should re-check in on the works in flight and ask, "Does what we are doing align to what we want to achieve in our vision?" Set the vision to be the north star: what you are aiming to achieve. You can define your own vision, but it could be something as simple as 'Find and remove waste at scale to improve delivery capacity and flow of products to our customers.'"

Finding and removing waste at scale isn't a quick win. It requires sticking to the vision (goal) and a form of commitment from the organisation.

The agile coaches embedding and scaling the vision in the work, will be continually reporting back on progress on how the vision is progressing.

STRATEGIC INTENT

Reaching out to the product owners and teams will allow you to find and remove waste at scale. You need to see what information is being captured now, and whether the leadership behaviours are suitable or not. How is the organisation measuring flow and waste (blockers).

PRODUCT INITIATIVE

Let's say that, having identified the challenges when looking at the strategic intent, you could see that the organisation had a majority of traditional leaders as opposed to digital minded leaders. Maturity may be low or non-existent and there may be little to no waste of knowledge to act upon. This is all OK in the early stages. It just shows you where the organisation is and provides a list of activities for your product backlog in order to start prioritising where to start and how to order the priority of the product backlog.

Each of these problems can be addressed either one at a time or collectively. Order the problems in terms of priority and start working through them with the aim of achieving the vision.

I was told many years ago when visiting Sydney, Australia. A guide told us that, a few years before, someone in Sydney wanted to lead paying tourists up and across the arch of the iconic Harbour Bridge. The local authorities said they would not allow such climbs, and presented 80-something objections why it could not happen (strategic intent). The person who wanted to operate the bridge tours then overcame all 80 challenges by creating a problem statement to be solved for each one. Now, Sydney has a bridge walk that is open to tourists.[32]

---

[32]   https://www.bridgeclimb.com/

It's by looking at the organisation and the challenges that you can create problem statements and work through them to embed finding and finding and removing waste to achieve the vision.

One method to come up with a problem statement, is to use a technique called CATWOE. Where you would consider aspects of the customer, actors, the transformation process, word view, owner and environment to form a problem statement. [33]

OPTIONS

Now that you have a set of problems to resolve in order to achieve the vision, these can be broken down into activities for the parties involved. They will need to find and experiment with different ways of achieving the vision, delivering a piece at time to resolve the strategic puzzle of finding and removing waste at scale.

CONTINUOUS PRODUCT DEVELOPMENT

Having established the vision, understand the challenges and have drawn up problem statements, we now have options to work through on our mission to find and remove waste. The vision and strategic intent have given us the product initiative and challenges.

By looking at the system of change in the form of The Waste Detectives Methods being embedded in its current status, we could start to set out the next increment to the product.

Working through the options and delivering the results and measuring how successful we have been at achieving that goal. Once we have done this, we would repeat this phase again.

---

[33] https://www.mindtools.com/aj9s8d7/the-catwoe-checklist

MEASURING SUCCESS

The Waste Detectives Methods and techniques highlighted the fact that as much as 50-70% of capacity is wasted in your system of change, value stream, lab and team. Now we are looking to create the ability for your organisation to remove waste. For more on this, see chapter 5.

The knowledge repository we discussed highlights how we can visualise the waste via counting the number of days lost and percentage of waste.

Removing all of the waste might never happen. But you can create an initiative to go after the waste and then measure the success against it, such as:

We believe that by finding and removing waste in our system of change we can reduce the amount of waste in the system from 70 to 50% down to 50 to 30%

Then via modelling of the waste and value flow data, and using the information building up in the knowledge repository, it will allow you to measure how successful you are at finding and removing waste.

METRICS

The metrics you use for measuring success will demonstrate how well the methods are working for you in the system of change. These measures will be the lagging measures once the method and capabilities are in place.

Leading measures of how capable your organisation is at finding and removing waste can be captured in the maturity capability, as seen in chapter 6. There will be a lag in the time new work that has entered and exited the system. The lagging measure will be the view of how the platform, lab, team is now performing with the waste removed. In order to get a view of this lagging measure, you need all work that was previously impacted by that type of waste you have just removed, to exit the system of change.

So look at both measures when measuring success:

1. The leading measure from the maturity capability.
2. The lagging measure from the waste knowledge repository. (How the Platform, lab, Team is performing in terms of waste)

HEART

Another way to measure how well the finding and removing waste is working is to consider the acronym HEART by Kerry Rodden: [34]

- Happiness - How happy are the consumers of finding and removing waste methods and concepts within the organisation?
- Engagement - How engaged are the communities, teams, labs and leaders in finding and removing waste?
- Adoption - What are the adoption rates in teams, labs and value streams in finding and removing waste?
- Retention - Of the areas that have used the finding and removing waste method, how many are still using it?
- Task Success - How many areas have found and removed waste to increase capacity?

The above areas could be measured and used to see the growth rate and stickability of methods and frameworks for finding and removing

---

[34] https://kerryrodden.com/heart/

waste. Adoption would be the leading measure, and Task Success the lagging measure.

HOW A CTO CAN USE THESE TECHNIQUES

Establish a team focusing on building a product to aid the storing and decision making from the waste data, linked to flow data to be available to all those working in the transformation of the organisation.

PRACTICAL STORY

Over a period of time having created The Waste Detectives Methods, using the techniques in this book. A waste knowledge repository of data and ways of work across the organisation strategically was developed. It was a pleasure to see this establishing itself and then grow organically throughout the organisation. Resistance was received along the way, but using techniques on influencing that were covered at the start of the book. These were overcome to establish an internal product to find and remove waste.

SUMMARY

In this chapter we have looked at how having someone in a product management-style role can aid the journey to find and remove waste at scale. We explored both good and bad characteristics of the type of person who would be a useful asset and suitable for you in this role. We looked at the need for a product manager for finding and removing waste at scale to establish the vision / purpose / goal of the organisation. Their view of the customer should include empathy and the ability to influence and tell stories. We then looked at the Knowledge Gap, Alignment Gap and Effects Gap.

Finally, we set the vision and strategic outcome, and showed how they define the work to be addressed in increments.

TAKEAWAYS

⇨ Be clear on your goal and stay on message.
⇨ Pick a product manager with the right behaviours.
⇨ Pick a product manager who is open minded.
⇨ Know the Gaps (Knowledge, Alignment and Effects).
⇨ Define the vision, strategic intent, product initiative and options.

CHAPTER 10
STORYTELLING

STORYTELLING ALLOWS YOU AS A CTO to maintain the growing influence on how important finding and removing waste is to the organisation. The techniques are covered in the next chapter, and will provide a guide of concepts to keep telling the story of finding and removing waste.

The chapter covers a number of storytelling techniques that are available and considers the pro's and con's

KEY CONCEPTS

Storytelling is the ability to build up the branding about the journey you are trying to achieve. The goal of the storytelling is to influence and change the behaviours of the digital minded leaders you are working with.

The most popular brands leverage storytelling. Companies such as Airbnb have introduced this in the product for customers to tell the stories of their experiences. They use this to build the relationship between hosts and guests. Storytelling helps make brands instantly recognisable and aims to influence our behaviours. [35]

Figure : 10.1. Story Telling
Image by Trueffelpix / Shutterstock.com

This also impacts how individuals behave and can generate follow-ship. At first, the brand may not be recognisable and there may be resistance as it is not understood what it relates to. Remember Tony not wanting to buy jeans online. I was telling the story of how I'd bought jeans online and how I found it useful. I was driven by the low price point and the fact that walking around shops is an experience I'd prefer to avoid at all costs.

The way you tell a story aids the influence of the brand. I was telling the jeans story to Tony from the problems I faced in finding well-priced, nice jeans without physically going to the shops. But this wasn't a problem that Tony had. He had a good job and was flush with money. He was able to pay what the vendor wanted and actually enjoyed going to the shops. So even though, in my eyes, online shopping was a great idea, I hadn't told the story in a way that resonated with Tony.

If I had known that he wanted to spend more quality time with his partner, and that the time he spent going to the shops reduced, I would have been able to tell Tony about buying jeans online in a language he'd hear and acknowledge.

---

[35] https://www.airbnb.co.uk/resources/hosting-homes/t/host-stories-5

Knowing what is important to the customer of the product, and who you are trying to influence, will help you establish the language and how you tell the story. Remember that the brand that you want to influence is finding and removing waste.

Everywhere in life there are brands, from the well-known (Amazon, Twitter and Coca-Cola) to our personal brand. This is what we are remembered by and our unique selling point in terms of what we offer in life and work. Being able to tell the story of finding and removing waste is a way of increasing your brand to deliver more products in less time as a chief technology officer (CTO).

WHAT ARE STORIES?

Stories are not just for books and movies. They are one of the most powerful marketing and influencing tools available; powerful forces to influence and connect. Stories are memorable because they stand out in a world of lacklustre messaging. Jerome Bruner's research shows that facts are 20 times more likely to be remembered if they are part of a story. Stories connect the storyteller and the story listener. As you hear a story, you connect with the storyteller and then bring others onto the same page.

In order to be able to tell good stories, connect problems and how you are pursuing the problem.

The story problem that concerns us is the scale of capacity being lost to the organisation and the pursuit is the vision to find and remove waste at scale.

Timing is important, so don't tell the story too soon. They may not be ready for removing waste at scale. (Just like Tony wasn't ready for buying Jeans online)

Now let's look at the pursuit.

As a CTO, listen to what senior leaders and their reports are saying and note the words they are using. Then when preparing the story of how to remove waste at scale, bring in the language they used. When I studied to be a trainer, we used to call this term UCOW (Use Customers Own Words).

You need to paint a picture of the solution in their heads to show that you understand the problem they are facing now and tell the story of a better future.

Try to find a specific problem and type of person to base the story around. Then draw in specific obstacles and objections that could occur along the way. Pull in methods and techniques into the story to help. Provide hope that things will get better and that waste can be found and removed. Help them imagine a future with less waste and a more predictable flow of products to customers. A future in which motivated colleagues have less frustrating blocked (waste) work restricting them from delivering and making them put work down regularly and task switch.

To tell a good story you need to:

1. Know your digital leader's problem and how removing waste can help with that problem.
2. Paint a picture they can remember and will recall when they think of you.
3. Propose a solution to fix their problem.

Then take the audience through the pain they are feeling now using the UCOW (Use Customers Own Words) technique. Leave the audience inspired that they resonate with those who want to buy into the technique of finding and removing waste. Then practise and listen each time you tell the story. Did it land and work? Did the digital minded leaders you are trying to influence get onboard and buy into the journey?

Storytelling helps presenting, vlogs and podcasts to be more effective. It connects the receivers of the story to the problem you are wanting to solve with them.

For further reading on storytelling, consider : The Laws of Brand Storytelling, Ekaterina Walter and Jessica Gioglio [36]

Strategies

1. Show you are human and you are the person behind the journey of finding and removing waste.
2. Tell the journey of where removing waste is now and what have you done in the past.
3. Experiment with the wording and story (listen and learn).
4. Share stories from those with the same problem. Tell stories of others on the journeys and describe success stories. Create quotes and inspiration messages.
5. Leverage stories from within the organisation about areas that are finding and removing waste.

TECHNIQUES TO TELL THE STORIES

Every interaction and person you speak to on the journey presents an opportunity to tell the story of finding and removing waste. It could be a chat at the coffee machine, a meeting in the lift, an inquiry about what you are working on, or the formal setting of a presentation. Each interaction is an opportunity to listen and test the message of the storytelling to increase the brand and the willingness to find and remove waste.

You may be able to adapt the language to incorporate those words to help the storytelling land the brand message and provide even more influence in the future.

---

[36] The Laws of Brand Storytelling, Ekaterina Walter and Jessica Gioglio

PRESENTING FACE TO FACE

A great way to speak to a large audience and tell a story in one sitting about your vision.

This will provide the ability for the audience to hear and see you present and an opportunity to potentially answer questions during and after the session. This could be in small groups or teams or to a much wider conference-style event.

Pros and Cons

Pro

- Ability to know who you have presented to.
- Feel how the message has landed.
- Sense the feedback and listen to the language you hear, to help adjust the story using customers' own words in the future.

Cons

- Travel and time for all colleagues to attend at the same time.

PRESENTING ONLINE (VIDEO AND VOICE)

Having a few people in the session with different roles might be helpful, such as someone to pick up questions in the chat whilst you are presenting, and other meeting-management tasks such as putting attendees on mute.

This can be achieved by using technologies such as Zoom or other video meeting or conference technologies.

Pros and Cons

Pros

- Ability to know who you have presented to.
- Feel how the message has landed.
- Ability to have questions answered in a chat and via voice personally.
- No travel costs and easier to set up.
- Ability to cover a large area, even whole countries and cities.

Cons

- Harder to read the room and sense the audience feedback when presenting.

VLOGS / PODCASTS

Record bite-sized clips of, say 15 minutes, with a bit of a jingle at the start. It's fairly quick to add to and you can build up your brand over time, episode-by-episode. As an example, see *The Waste Detective Diaries podcast*. [37]

Pros and Cons

Pros

- Simple to create and a way to build up over time.
- Allow individuals to listen or watch in their own time.

---

[37] https://open.spotify.com/episode/1OYOF6vcSxZdKNzS92M8PQ?si=YyukWSNmShWK40BpqArrSw&nd=1

- Ability to bring in different guests and different perspectives to help grow the brand and awareness.

Cons

- Only a digital footprint. Requires someone to find and play the recording in a saturated market of podcasts and blogs.
- Not a personal connection with the listener so it is difficult to gauge response and feedback that will help you.

BLOGS

The blogs can be used to post about how things are progressing with finding and removing waste, then examples from teams and labs about their stories of finding and removing waste.

Pros and Cons

Pro

- Easy to start.
- Having a blog page provides a reason for those you are trying to influence to return to the website.
- Ability to create a community feel and sense of being around the subject.
- Keeps an achievement of the journey via new and historic stories.

Cons

- Time commitment to regularly update.

BUILDING THE STORY

In *The Laws of Brand Storytelling*, (2018), Ekaterina Walter and Jessica Gioglio discuss some of the rules of crafting a story.

You're likely to do this via many media routes. When the same message is being landed, it saves ambiguity and noise that could prevent the goal you are trying. So say what you are doing, and speak from experience. Explain how the consumer of finding waste will benefit from it and what it will feel like on the journey. In terms of simplicity, follow the KISS principle (Keep It Simple Stupid). We all have busy lives, so the simpler the message, the better.

> *"Over 60% of employees are considered brand champion in companies perceived to be simple, versus 20% in companies that are perceived complex."*

Let's look at their "laws" here and see how they relate to telling the story of finding and removing waste.

The Laws of Brand Storytelling,
Ekaterina Walter and Jessica Gioglio

The language we use is important. The more you use the Customers' Own Words (UCOW) and language, the more they can relate. In the past, when I told the story at a senior level, I used the language of waste and capacity lost. However, this came across in a negative way. The person did indeed have a problem with capacity and costs. But turning the language around to talk about the opportunity and the ability to find more capacity with no more money was more positive and allowed them to buy in. The leader in this instance was trying to find a way to sell the concept to their reports. Telling the story in the right language and tone allows it to be portable and told via others so that they can draw attention to the current problems.

Use visuals when telling the story, but keep it simple, with a limited amount of text.

> *"People can recall 65 percent of the visual content that they see almost 3 days later, compared to 10 percent of written content"*
>
> The Laws of Brand Storytelling,
> Ekaterina Walter and Jessica Gioglio

If you have modelled the amount of waste in the organisation, which could be in the region of 50-70%, you may want to pull in the volume of waste in the system of change value stream, lab or team to generate some urgency. For example, you are losing X number of days per year in work not flowing through the system versus Y days of value flow delivery. This could potentially be a big number and could be used to generate urgency. This will make it real. It makes it more likely that the organisation wants to, and is ready to, act on removing waste.

SUMMARY

Jerome Bruner's research shows that facts are 20 times more likely to be remembered if they are part of a story by connecting the storyteller and listener.

You can use a variety of channels to reach a wider audience. Listen to the words they use as this may be an opportunity to adjust your language to theirs. Customers like hearing their own language so using the UCOW (Use Customers' Own Words) will help land the story journey and build brand awareness of what you are trying to do.

Try to understand a digital leader's problem and how removing waste can help with that problem. Paint a picture that they can remember and repeat when they think of you. Most importantly, propose a solution to fix their problem. This allows the story to work for both your customer and the methods and techniques you are trying to influence in your mission.

In terms of storytelling, start by testing the story and measure it to see how successfully it's landed. Learn from what you did the first time and then improve the story.

When presenting in whatever format, smile, enjoy it, and listen to emotions.

HOW A CTO CAN USE THESE TECHNIQUES

Encourage your agile coaches and scrum masters who are embedding the waste detective method to keep telling the story and be available to those who have questions on the method.

PRACTICAL STORY

Having devised and built The Waste Detectives Methods, I have used all of the techniques above, my personal favourite is face to face or via a video call, as that allows me as a storyteller to interact with the audience and field questions on the method. I do like doing podcasts, however a typical feedback loop from a podcast is a thumbs up that for me doesn't provide me with a lot of feedback on how to improve the message for the next story telling session.

TAKEAWAYS

- ⇨ Stories build connections.
- ⇨ Stories connect you as a CTO and the agile coaches and scrum masters working for you to the problem you are trying to solve. (Finding and removing waste)
- ⇨ The more stories you tell, the more connections you are going to make.

REFERENCES

Chapter 1

- Block Buster - https://en.wikipedia.org/wiki/Blockbuster_(retailer)
- *Coin Game* - https://www.youtube.com/watch?v=fh4nkQnWL6I
- Brian Hooker and Richard Moir, (2022), The Waste Detectives
- Dominica DeGrandis, (2015), *Making Work Visible : Exposing Time Theft to Optimize Work & Flow.*
- Jill Duffy (2016), 'How Much Time Do We Lose Task-Switching?', Productivity Report: Bridging Research And Practice On Personal Productivity. [https://productivityreport.org/2016/02/22/how-much-time-do-we-lose-task-switching/]
- DR A.J Drenth. (2013), The 16 Personality Types
- Geoff Watts, (2017), Product Mastery
- George Green (2021), The Art of Influencing People,
- Danial S. Vacanti, (2015), Actionable Agile Metrics for Predictability

Chapter 2

- https://quixy.com/blog/digital-leadership/

- https://www.cuscalpayments.com.au/news/videos/dbs-incredible-digital-transformation-with-paul-cobban/
- https://www.productlessons.xyz/article/why-amazon-fire-phone-failed-case-study
- https://techcrunch.com/2022/11/09/elon-musk-details-his-vision-for-a-twitter-payments-system/?guccounter=1&guce_referrer=aHR0cHM6Ly93d3cuZ29vZ2xlLmNvbS8&guce_referrer_sig=AQAAAGu2q2jLHUwnK6zZGzOT89a0SvFYPBT-9abehuTbDE-K0dCCvEFzUsk-erkqf0C8cpnAOtRk1VPTpEkiN-lyUqe5jgkjPZeRGfPVwGmrkTLppomUvbyYUSFAF0xED8XB2gCZ83lcAAkaYByThqTo7g-5Fv0HxfmZu8ldmPLXu08u
- https://deming.org/
- https://nanoglobals.com/glossary/scientific-management-theory-of-frederick-taylor/
- Brian Hooker and Richard Moir, (2022), The Waste Detectives
- Ram Charan and Raj B. Vattikuti (2022), The Digital Leader Finding Faster More Profitable Path To Exceptional Growth
- John Seddon (2019), Performance in Beyond Command and Control
- Mathew Skelton and Manuel Pais, (2019), Team Topologies

Chapter 3

- https://productivityreport.org/2016/02/22/how-much-time-do-we-lose-task-switching/
- Brian Hooker and Richard Moir (2022), The Waste Detectives Methods and Techniques
- Mik Kersten, *(2018), Project to Product*
- Jeff Sutherland, (2015), *The Art of Doing Twice the Work in Half the Time*

Chapter 4
- https://www.investopedia.com/ask/answers/021115/what-difference-between-capital-expenditure-and-revenue-expenditure.asp
- https://agiledictionary.com/209/spike/
- Man on the Moon - Youtube : https://www.youtube.com/watch?v=7zLWGGZQQVw
- https://www.investopedia.com/ask/answers/021115/what-difference-between-capital-expenditure-and-revenue-expenditure.asp

Chapter 5
- Chapter 3 - Waste Detectives Method
- https://www.scrum.org/resources/blog/user-story-or-stakeholder-story
- https://www.scrum.org/resources/blog/simple-example-definition-done#:~:text=Acceptance%20criteria%20are%20an%20optional,%2C%20customer%2C%20or%20other%20stakeholder.
- https://deming.org/explore/pdsa/

Chapter 6
- https://en.wikipedia.org/wiki/Capability_Maturity_Model
- James R. Persse, (2001), Implementing the Capability Maturity Model,
- David J Anderson and Andy Carmichael, (2016), Essential kanban Condensed,
- John Seddon, (2019), Beyond Command and Control,

Chapter 7
- Matthew Skelton and Manuel Pais, (2019), Team Topologies
- Matthew Skelton and Manuel Pais, (2022), Teams Interactions Workbook,
- John Seddon, (2019), Beyond Command and Control

Chapter 8
- Chris Pearce, (2020), The Broken CEO

Chapter 9
- Melissa Perri, (2019), Escaping the Build Trap
- Stephen Bundy, (2011) author of The Knowledge Gap (from the art of action)

Chapter 10
- https://www.harvardbusiness.org/what-makes-storytelling-so-effective-for-learning/
- Visit Chapter 1: Influencing & Convincing of the importance
- https://open.spotify.com/episode/1OYOE6vcSxZdKNzS92M8PQ?si=YyukWSNmSh-WK40BpqArrSw&nd=1
- Ekaterina Walter and Jessica Gioglio, (2018), *The Laws of Brand Storytelling*

Can I ask a small favour?

It would mean a lot to me if you could spare a moment to review this book by clicking the link below. You only need to write a couple of sentences so it won't take long.

I'd be very grateful. By leaving a review, you'll help more people discover this book and learn about waste in their organisations. And as you can tell, I am passionate about waste and its causes and we really want to tell as many people as possible about it.

Thank you!
Brian

ABOUT THE AUTHOR

BRIAN HOOKER

Brian WORKS AS A BUSINESS AGILITY lead focused on transformation projects. He is the joint author of *The Waste Detectives*, published in 2022, a #1 bestseller in the IT Project Management category of the Kindle Store. He makes guest appearances on transformation-themed podcasts including Agile Amped (Accenture) and The Flow Community (Planview). [38]

He has a degree in computer science from the University of the West of England and experience in a wide range of transformation roles, from testing to system engineering, analysis, and transformational coaching.

Away from work, you're likely to find Brian in a wetsuit, bodyboarding at his nearest beach with his daughter. He is also a long-suffering fan of Plymouth Argyle F.C. (the Manchester United of the southwest, England).

---

[38] https://soundcloud.com/agile-amped-uk/the-waste-detectives-with-brian-hooker-and-richard-moir

Printed in Great Britain
by Amazon